REASON & ART
IN TEACHING
SECONDARY-SCHOOL ENGLISH

Reason
& Art
IN TEACHING
SECONDARY-SCHOOL ENGLISH

Morris Finder
Foreword by Ralph W. Tyler

Temple University Press
PHILADELPHIA

Temple University Press, Philadelphia 19122
© 1976 by Temple University. All rights reserved
Published 1976
Printed in the United States of America

International Standard Book Number: 0-87722-071-9
Library of Congress Catalog Card Number: 76-9554

Dec. 15, '76

To Natalie

CONTENTS

CONTENTS ix

TABLES

ACKNOWLEDGMENTS

It is a pleasure to acknowledge the sources I have drawn upon.

Although specific acknowledgments appear throughout, I must cite as indispensable *Basic Principles of Curriculum and Instruction* by Ralph W. Tyler; *The Languages of Criticism and the Structure of Poetry* by R. S. Crane; *Tragedy and the Theory of Drama* by Elder Olson; "Moral Universe and Dramatic Effect" by Bernard Weinberg (particularly in the writing of Chapter 6); and the following writings of John Dewey: "My Pedagogic Creed," "The Relation of Theory to Practice in Education," and *The Sources of a Science of Education*.

The State University of New York at Albany, particularly its School of Education, has been exceptionally cooperative: Joseph Leese and the Kettering Foundation supported some of the early formulations. Randolph S. Gardner, H. Craig Sipe, Gerald W. Snyder, and Peggy Weissleder have through the years arranged for clerical and typing assistance. The testing of materials in methods classes and in research seminars has been made possible by the services and resources of the mimeographing room of the School of Education, whose work is ably managed by Beverly Spiegel and her assistants. A sabbatical semester granted for the fall of 1972 was of much help as were the responses of students to the ideas presented.

The typing of successive drafts has been mainly the burden of graduate assistants. They are in order of service: Karen Johnsen, Susan Greenberg, Susan Jagendorf, Anna Yee, Barbara Gesang, Karen Sandell, and Clorinda Lisi. Miss Gesang, in addition, has edited some of the copy. Other graduate students who have contributed include Eleanor Brown, Lee Brown, William H. Cullen, Edwin W. Dietrick, David W. Maat, and Ralph Ware.

James E. Cochrane, my colleague in English education, has helped in several ways. He has tested materials, contributed to the writing, helped formulate some of the ideas, and been unstinting in his encouragement. Mary Elizabeth Grenander, my colleague in the Department of English, has been particularly helpful in formulating the "part-whole" skills.

Through discussion, teaching, writings, and correspondence, colleagues from other institutions have assisted in various ways: Harold B. Dunkel, Margaret Early, John I. Goodlad, Eric P. Hamp, J. N. Hook, Arnold Lazarus, David H. Richter, James H. Sledd, Ralph W. Tyler, and the late R. S. Crane.

And as always, my wife, to whom this book is dedicated, has contributed to the discussion, to the typing, and to the creation of the many conditions that made the completion of this book possible.

I am also grateful for permission to reprint the following selections:

Katharine Brush, "Birthday Party." Originally published in *The New Yorker*, XXII, No. 5 (March 16, 1946), 54. Reprinted by permission of Thomas S. Brush.

Robert Frost, "Dust of Snow." From *The Poetry of Robert Frost*, edited by Edward Connery Lathem. Copyright 1923, © 1969 by Holt, Rinehart and Winston. Copyright 1951 by Robert Frost. Reprinted by permission of Holt, Rinehart and Winston, Publishers, and Jonathan Cape Limited, holder of the British rights.

Fred J. Kulb, "Crime in Depression Years," *The New York Times*, October 20, 1970, p. 42. © 1970 by The New York Times Company. Reprinted by permission.

John Updike, "Ex-Basketball Player." From *The Carpentered Hen and Other Tame Creatures* by John Updike. Copyright © 1957 by John Updike. Originally appeared in *The New Yorker* and reprinted by permission of Harper & Row, Publishers, Inc., and Victor Gollancz Limited, holder of the British rights.

Tennessee Williams, *The Glass Menagerie*. From *The Glass Menagerie* by Tennessee Williams. Copyright 1945 by Tennessee Williams and Edwina D. Williams and renewed 1973 by Tennessee Williams. Reprinted by permission of Random House, Inc.

William Carlos Williams, "This Is Just to Say." From William Carlos Williams, *Collected Earlier Poems*. Copyright 1938 by New Directions Publishing Corporation. Reprinted by permission of New Directions Publishing Corporation.

FOREWORD

Ralph W. Tyler

The American public appears to have lost faith in the effectiveness of schooling. The press reports a continuing decline over the past dozen years in the average performance of high school seniors in the admission tests of the College Entrance Examination Board and the American College Testing Program. The greatest decline in score is reported for the verbal section of the Scholastic Aptitude Test. College teachers of English complain of the increasing number of entering students whose written composition is inadequate and whose reading skills are limited. The National Assessment of Educational Progress reports:

> In a survey of writing skills taken first in 1970 and repeated in 1974, National Assessment found that, in 1974, students aged 13 and 17 used a simpler vocabulary, wrote in a shorter, "primer-like" style and had more incoherent paragraphs than their counterparts in school four years earlier.[1]

The report went on to state that the essays of these students "showed that basic writing mechanics (punctuation, capitalization, agreement, spelling and word usage) taught in elementary and junior high school, were being handled adequately by a vast majority of the students. But there was a drastic drop in coherence and a trend toward more sentence fragments."

In commenting on this assessment, Richard Lloyd Jones of the University of Iowa and Chairman of the Conference on

College Composition and Communication said: "Our society provides less and less motivation for writing. Students question the need to master a skill they may never be called upon to use after school has ended."[2]

These are illustrations of the problems now faced by teachers of English. Many are reexamining their instructional programs and find that they lack a comprehensive and coherent conception of the role of language in modern society and the guiding principles for developing a sound program of instruction. The recent work of scholars in linguistics, literary criticism, and social linguistics has brought new understanding of the processes involved in composition and in the comprehension and interpretation of literature. At the same time, as programs of curriculum reconstruction have been instituted throughout the world, systematic procedures for curriculum development and instructional planning have been formulated.

Little of this, however, has touched the teaching of English in secondary schools. Courses in methods of teaching high-school English have not generally considered recent scholarship in language and literature, nor have they shown the usefulness of a rationale for curriculum development and instructional planning. This book fills the void. It presents a comprehensive program for the teaching of literature and language, a program that incorporates the work of scholars in the several relevant disciplines and employs an effective procedure for curriculum planning and instruction.

One of the reasons for the very limited application to teaching that has been made of recent research in linguistics and literary criticism is the fact that this research has been published in technical reports and not been made familiar or even understandable to the high-school English teacher, nor to most undergraduate teachers. Furthermore, although in curriculum development, in the psychology of learning, and in testing and evaluation, experiment and experience have furnished a base for a new teaching rationale, much of this recent work has gone unpublished. This book brings these diverse elements together into a conception of English teaching not presented elsewhere. It explains a procedure for the teacher that puts theory into practice.

For more than twenty years, Morris Finder has been teaching English and preparing teachers of English in widely differing situations—Chicago; the Philippines; Afghanistan; Bellingham, Washington; and the State University of New York at Albany. He has been formulating, testing, and revising his ideas about the teaching of English composition and the interpretation of literature until they are sound, coherent, and practical. They are set forth in this book clearly and in an orderly fashion. The explanations are helpful and the illustrative exercises are very useful. The logic and rhetoric clearly refute the lofty view of the academic scholar that methods courses can have no real substance. Its logical rationale and its comprehensiveness will appeal to college and university teachers who seek an intellectual foundation for their work. It will also be respected by professors of English because it recognizes the important contributions that English can make to the education of the high-school student if the curriculum design and the instructional practices are appropriately developed.

If, however, the book is to serve English teachers most helpfully, it must be read and reread with careful attention to its comprehensive rationale. It is not an easy guide, for it demands that English teaching be treated as a profession with a purpose and a clearly formulated set of principles. It is not a painless recipe for "handling" high-school English. But when read with care and reflection, and when the ideas thus obtained are employed in the planning of the English program and in instruction, this book is very rewarding.

Notes

1. *NAEP Newsletter,* 8, No. 6 (Dec. 1975), 1.
2. *Ibid.,* p. 3.

REASON & ART
IN TEACHING
SECONDARY-SCHOOL ENGLISH

INTRODUCTION

Although "reason" and "art" appear in its title, this book is longer on reason than it is on art. To explain this emphasis is to tell what the book intends to do.

Purpose

There are principles of teaching and there are principles of subject matter. The teacher brings the two together. I use "reason" to refer to the principles and "art" to refer to their use. Although the book explains the principles, their use depends largely upon situations within particular classes.

A single purpose, therefore, determines the content of this text: the reader's active control of the principles. Such control is the foundation for intelligence and flexibility in teaching and, thereby, for its practice as an art.

Content and organization

I express the principles as sets of skills that define planning and teaching. Because a statement of ends or skills will usually not be understood unless illustrated by means through which these are achieved, examples and exercises appear throughout.

Not only are the principles the basis of intelligent teaching, they are, unfortunately, accessible to misunderstanding and misuse. Readers, therefore, must be warned. The warnings

3

are issued in a section called "Pitfalls," placed near the end of each chapter.

Chapter 1 introduces a set of terms and distinctions with which planning and teaching are discussed throughout the book. The chapter is based explicitly on Ralph W. Tyler's method of inquiry into problems of curriculum and instruction.

Chapter 2 discusses the comprehension of expository prose. There are particular properties of such prose, and skills of comprehension are inferred from these properties. For example, an argument says something; it may, therefore, be comprehended as literal statement. An argument, further, affects readers, which implies that it may be comprehended as a means of producing its intended effects. These two kinds of comprehension are discussed in Chapter 2.

Chapter 3 is a supplement to Chapter 1, where evaluation is among the terms introduced. Using the skills of comprehension introduced in Chapter 2, the third chapter examines evaluation and its uses more closely.

Chapter 4 explores the comprehension of argument further. Not only does an argument say something and affect readers, it exhibits a process of reasoning. This third aspect of comprehension has traditionally been called the "analysis of ideas." The fourth chapter, then, identifies the skills and shows their uses not only in comprehension but in everyday living, independent study, and curricular innovation.

Having treated three aspects of comprehending expository and argumentative prose, the book continues in Chapter 5 with the writing of such forms. The topics discussed include the operational principles of writing, the correspondence of the skills of writing to those of comprehension, evaluation as a means to improved composition, and procedures by which students may learn to evaluate each other's writing.

Chapter 6 discusses some basic elements of literary works and is the first of three chapters on the teaching of literature. Further, Chapter 6 examines relationships among the emotional and other effects of literature, the values built into literary works, and the ethical and moral assumptions of the reader. Adolescents may examine and clarify their ethical beliefs, their aspirations, and their problems through discussing these relationships.

The ideas developed in the sixth chapter are extended in Chapter 7 to lyric poetry and in Chapter 8 to drama and fiction. Problems of censorship and the selection of longer literary works also are treated in Chapter 8.

Chapter 9 discusses language not as an instrument of communication, not as the material out of which verbal discourses are constructed, but rather as a distinctive subject of study. In a sense, such an inquiry is similar to the study of the number system in arithmetic and mathematics classes. The subject of Chapter 9 implies a distinction between objectives suited to linguistic topics and those suited to composition. Failures to understand that distinction are common and result in much pointless and confused teaching. Further, the chapter explains and illustrates, step by step, the procedures by which aspects of linguistics or of any other subject may be rationally and systematically incorporated into classroom work.

Underlying theory

The principles that the reader is expected to control stem from a particular theory. The starting points are these: Reading, writing, and teaching are activities for achieving purposes. Similarly, works of literature and expository prose are made things for achieving purposes. Their purposes determine what these activities and things are. A chair, for example, is intended to seat one person. That intention determines its form and the materials it is made of.

To explain further: An ax is intended as a tool to slice through wood. To achieve that intention, its form must be a wedged edge with a handle attached. Its purpose, then, not only determines its being a wedged edge, it determines also the work that the axmaker must do and the kinds of materials he must use. Any problem about the ax itself, therefore, must entail its purpose, its form, its manufacture, or its material; and such a problem may imply any combination or all of these four principles of construction.

To some readers, the foregoing discussion may sound

familiar. They would recognize it as an explanation of Aristotle's four causes. To clarify these underlying principles let me express in different words the constructive causes by which our ax is brought into being: *Purpose or final cause:* To slice through wood. *The form to be made or formal cause:* A wedged edge with an attached handle. *The work of the maker or efficient cause:* The indispensable minimum of tasks, common to all axmakers, that are needed to produce the ax. *The materials to be used or material cause:* Steel and wood.

As suggested, not only is the construction of an ax accessible to explanation by the four causes, but so is any practical activity or made thing. The made things may include poems, stories, and arguments. The material that these things are made out of is language or words.

I assume that a relatively small number of questions implied by the four causes may be used to organize and, in a sense, unify the teaching of English. At the same time these constructive principles facilitate a coherent understanding of the immense diversity of the English curriculum. I justify this contention by the following line of reasoning.

The unity and diversity of actions and things may be explained by the four principles of construction. Actions and things, teaching and discourses are unified in the sense that they have purposes or final causes and, related to these, formal, efficient, and material causes. Actions and things are diversified in the sense that, although their constructive principles are similar, the uniqueness of every individual argument, work of literature, instance of teaching, and every other purposeful activity or thing may be explained by these principles. All such examples of uniqueness are differences in purposes, forms, making or doing, and materials. With the four causes as underlying explanation, this book makes explicit the particular principles both of teaching and of such subject matter as expository prose, imaginative literature, and selected linguistic topics.

Needs

The text is suited to meet at least five kinds of needs. One, just discussed, is for an explicit formulation of the principles.

A second need, related to the first, is for improving the achievement of all learners. To bring this about, we must clarify and justify what is to be learned, and devise activities through which the students, whoever they may be, will acquire that learning. The entire text addresses that problem. Although students who are at least average are usually depicted in illustrations of learning activities, the principles may be adapted to the less able and the more able.

A controversial word, "accountability," suggests a third need that the text may supply. Regardless of the meaning that one may attach to accountability, the practice of keeping the administration and the community informed about the progress of instruction has for years been recognized as sound. When the administration and the public know about desirable programs, these stand a chance of receiving continuous support. Because this book provides materials for explicating the ends and means of the teaching of English, it clarifies the information that may be conveyed.

Another controversial term, "competence-performance" in teacher education, implies a fourth need. The supplying of that need, however, does not imply uncritical acceptance of every so-called "competence-performance" scheme for preparing teachers. But competence-performance may remind educators that the justification for any program of education is the achievement of its learners. Because this book is organized around such expected achievement, it suggests specific principles by which to prepare teachers of English.

Finally, the text may be viewed as a contribution to research in the teaching of English. In *The Sources of a Science of Education*, Dewey explains that (1) the purpose of research in education is increased intelligence and flexibility in everyday practice, (2) educational practice provides the problems for research, and (3) any method that enables systematic inquiry into a problem is a valid research method.

The book presents terms, distinctions, and methods aimed at systematic inquiry into problems of reading, writing, and their teaching. Therefore, the terms and methods become instruments of research when used to solve an educational problem. An example may clarify. Chapter 2 presents a set of skills for comprehending expository and argumentative prose, and Chapter 5, the corresponding skills of writing. Teaching to write exposition and argument is an abiding educational problem. The two chapters cited, as well as the chapter on evaluation (Chapter 3), may be used to inquire into the following hypothesis: "Improvement in skills of comprehension influences improvement in the corresponding skills of writing." Such a study is likely to arrive at new knowledge about the problem and, therefore, at increased enlightenment for the teacher of English.

Possible uses

Having cited some needs that the text may fill, let me suggest where in the curriculum the book may fill these needs and, perhaps, others.

Because it treats the first principles of the profession, the book is appropriate to basic courses in English-teaching methodology. Because these first principles are not widely understood, some teachers of methodology may feel that the text belongs at more advanced levels. However that may be, I have been using mimeographed versions of the text in both undergraduate and graduate courses. In my opinion, the first principles should be taught as early as possible and whenever needed. When the book is used in any course or in-service program, it may be supplemented with poems, plays, stories, argumentative prose, or any other kind of content suitable to secondary-school English.

Although the book makes no attempt to treat all subjects that may be considered appropriate to English, it does describe procedures through which any subject or discipline may be incorporated into the curriculum. Chapter 4 explains a method by which scholarship may be analyzed for its possible contributions to school learning. Chapter 1 presents a method by which such potential contributions may be translated into a program of instruction. As mentioned, this process of analysis and curricular innovation is illustrated in Chapter 9.

Typically, student teachers and students in methods courses are required to observe teaching. The ideas presented in this book may be useful in guiding observation, particularly if the student observes, as Dewey argues he should, not to learn how the good teacher does it, but rather to find out how to analyze a learning activity for the properties that make it good, bad, or indifferent.

Similarly, the book should be useful in student teaching, which, Dewey suggests, should be a means for increasing the student's understanding of the principles of teaching, and not primarily a means for developing techniques of classroom management. I assume that the principles of teaching and of education generally are those explained throughout Chapter 1 and formulated in the section "The Capabilities of Teaching."

Hints for comprehending the book

The book has been written to be read sequentially from beginning to end; earlier chapters give background for understanding later ones. Also, my experience suggests that the typical student will not control the ideas and methods unless his participation goes beyond the reading and discussion of the text. Exercises, therefore, appear throughout. Further, the chapters on the comprehension of exposition and argument (Chapters 2 and 4) may guide the reader to the comprehension of this text, and the glossary entries may be read as restatements of the major ideas presented.

A note on pronouns

Throughout, I use the pronoun *I* with its usual meaning. The pronoun *we* is intended to convey the sense of reader and writer considering a matter together. Also, I use *we* to refer to competent readers of literature. For reasons of style, I follow the convention of using masculine pronouns to refer to human nouns that imply both sexes: *teacher, student,* and *rhetorician,* for example.

CHAPTER 1

OBJECTIVES AND PLANS

Responsible teaching implies objectives and rational procedures for their attainment. This chapter, then, discusses the nature and formulation of objectives and their uses in planning, teaching, and evaluating.

The nature of objectives

A simple chain of reasoning explains the teacher's need for objectives. Because teaching is intended to bring about changes in what learners are able to do, know, understand, appreciate, and prefer, the objectives of teaching are the changes that learners are to acquire.[1] If the teacher is to choose objectives wisely, he must know how to justify these. If he is to teach well, he must know how to use objectives in planning, conducting, and evaluating a program of instruction. This book intends to clarify these issues as they relate to the teaching of English in secondary schools.

It is useful to distinguish objectives at four degrees of generality.[2] At a highly generalized level, there are aims proposed for all of education. I call these Level 1 objectives. Here are some examples:

In a society of free men, the proper aim of education is to prepare the individual to make wise decisions. All else is but contributory.[3]

The purpose of education is to stimulate and guide . . . self-development.[4]

The purpose which runs through and strengthens all other educational purposes—the common thread of education—is the development of the ability to think.[5]

At a somewhat less generalized level there are objectives that are widely accepted for English. I call these objectives Level 2. The examples include:

Appreciate and understand literature.

Read and write.

Understand the English language.

For the classroom teacher, such intentions as these must be translated into statements that express more clearly what students are able to do when, for example, they "understand literature." I call such statements Level 3 objectives. Here are some examples of Level 3 statements that are consistent with the Level 2 objective "Appreciate and understand literature."

State the literal sense of what is going on in a lyric poem.

Explain the aspect of human experience that a short story depicts.

Identify the emotional effect upon the reader that a play is intended to produce.

Finally, Level 4 objectives are the same as Level 3 except that we substitute for such words as "lyric poem," "novel," or "play," the titles of particular works or other specific examples of content:

State the literal sense of what is going on in "Anthem for Doomed Youth."

Explain the aspect of human experience that "The Cask of Amontillado" depicts.

Identify the emotional effect that *The Glass Menagerie* is intended to produce.

Level 3 and 4 objectives may not always convey their intentions to everyone. An everyday analogy explains why: The context clarifies the meaning of a word. Similarly, the context of thought and discussion through which objectives have been derived explicates their meanings. To separate objectives from their context of thought and discussion is like citing a passage without reference to its context. For the objective "Identify the plots of short stories," the meaning of "plot" must be ascertained before anyone can tell what the objective means. And "plot," I must add, is used in differing senses. The Level 3 and 4 objectives in this chapter, then, are cited not so much to convey a specific intention of teaching as to illustrate a useful way in which to state objectives.

In a sense, the term "Level 4 objective" is misleading. The real objective is not Level 4 but Level 3. Level 4 specifies particular lyric poems, stories, essays, and so forth. We use such particular works and other kinds of content for teaching to comprehend and appreciate lyric poetry in general, the wide range of short stories, and the limitless number of arguments and articles. Level 3 identifies the general classes of content of which desired learning is a part. Put another way, we teach "Ozymandias" as a means of teaching the comprehension of all the poems within the students' range of comprehension.

There is another reason for drawing this distinction. We have at our disposal vast numbers of poems, plays, works of fiction, topics for composition, and so on. There are no sacrosanct lists of these that must be used if students are to acquire the learning specified by Level 3 objectives.

Some stories or other kinds of content are more suited or otherwise attractive to some teachers and students than they are to others. The disadvantaged will have a hard time making sense out of the summer-resort customs of Ring Lardner's "I Can't Breathe," but will enjoy his story "Haircut." Yet one class reading "I Can't Breathe" and another reading "Haircut" may both be acquiring the same skills of comprehension. Thus, the distinction between Levels 3 and 4 encourages adaptability of content to particular teachers, groups, and individuals.

Notice that in the statements of Levels 3 and 4 such words as these *do not appear:* "understand," "be aware of," "recognize," "gain insight into," "grasp the significance of," "improve," "know," "learn," "realize," "study," "think," and so on. Such words, rather vague in reference, are perfectly good to help one get started. They belong not at Levels 3 or 4, but at Levels 1 or 2.

The demands of practical teaching require that we clarify just what a student is doing when he "understands," for example, lyric poetry. Is he stating the literal sense of what is going on in the poem? Explaining how it reflects the times in which it was written? Explaining what emotions it is intended to arouse? Is he doing some combination of these things or others? Such words as "understand" and "gain insight into" becloud and, at the most, suggest rather than clarify.

To help clarify, it is useful to *begin* with such a vague notion as "understand" and then ask, "What is a learner doing when he "understands."

To help the reader formulate instructional or Level 3 objectives, I offer a short list of verbs. It is likely that the following list is sufficient to begin just about all statements of Levels 3 and 4 for English that are accessible to direct, specific instruction:

compare	explain	speak
contrast	formulate	state
describe	identify	summarize
distinguish	infer	write

The two aspects of objectives

A usefully stated Level 3 or 4 objective may be viewed as a statement consisting of two aspects. The first may be called "behavioral"; such words as "describe," "explain," and "identify" constitute for an objective its behavioral aspect. The second aspect, called "content," refers to such parts of learning as literature, exposition, argument, grammar, and to various aspects of these such as the literal sense of what is going on in lyric poems, the relationships between deep and surface grammatical structure, the intended effects upon the reader of an editorial, the main proposition of what is read, or the main proposition to be conveyed in an expository or argumentative composition.

For the objective "Explain the literal sense of what is going on in lyric poems," the word "explain" specifies the behavioral aspect and "the literal sense of what is going on in lyric poems," the content.

The list includes the words "speak" and "write" but not "listen" and "read." The Level 3 objective "Write 300-word essays on literary topics" necessarily and desirably implies much freedom and latitude. The same argument applies to an objective such as "Speak fluently in everyday conversation." For such objectives as these a necessary freedom implies a necessary ambiguity.

But the statement "Read 300-word essays on contemporary topics" is as ambiguous as if the word "understand" were substituted for "read." To avoid the ambiguity of "read," write statements describing what the student is expected to be able to do as a result of his reading. Then arrive at Level 3 objectives. Some examples follow:

Identify the main ideas in essays.

Infer political bias in newspaper editorials.

Distinguish fact from opinion in magazine articles.

Summarize arguments in essays.

Write as many objectives as needed to convey explicitly what "understand" is taken to mean. The same argument applies to listening: a counterpart to the first objective listed above is "Identify main ideas in informative speeches." In the four chapters that follow I discuss in some detail the problems of reading and writing exposition and argument.

Notice that Level 3 objectives are always expressed as the learning that students are to acquire. It is wrong-headed to state such objectives as what the teacher is to do. The purpose of education is not to put teachers to work but to help students learn.

Distinguishing ends and means

I must warn against confusing an objective with a learning activity or an evaluative item. An instructional objective (Level 3) in this view is a generally useful capability that can be defended as worth having. (Later in this chapter I discuss the grounds for justifying objectives.) "Identify main arguments in three out of five essays" is a learning activity or an item of evaluation. "Improvise a scene of a play" is certainly not an objective but a learning activity, as is "Write a character sketch."

Objectives as a means to professional freedom

Throughout this book I explain and illustrate the use of objectives in the teaching of particular kinds of content. By "use of objectives" I do not imply that a task of this book is to present a set of objectives and activities for students to imitate. Rather, my purpose is to provide prospective and practicing teachers with methods of thinking by which they can plan and teach in whatever situation they may be. Only exceptionally gifted people can rely on their intuitions and common sense and still teach well. In this book I intend to convey what the gifted teacher does intuitively and to present this knowledge as explicit and systematic methods of inquiry.

It is a mistake to suppose that systematized inquiry puts teachers and students into a straitjacket and inhibits their freedom. Instead, as John Dewey has noted:

Command of scientific methods and systematized subject-matter liberates individuals; it enables them to see new problems, devise new procedures, and in general makes for diversification rather than for set uniformity. But at the same time these diversifications have a cumulative effect in an advance shared by all workers in the field.[6]

I have already given an example of the sense in which systematized procedures of inquiry liberates: When we have justified and stated as an objective, "Explain the literal sense of what is going on in short stories," we are free to select stories suited to the interests and backgrounds of the class; we are free to select or devise any set of activities that are likely to help our students acquire that learning; we are free to organize the activities in an order that is likely to help bring about the desired learning more efficiently; and we are free to select or devise situations by which we may evaluate the achievements of our students and, thereby, the success of our teaching.

Clarity of goal: Arguments and counterarguments

There is, however, much misunderstanding of, and even hostility toward, systematized procedures of thinking and doing. The practice of specifying objectives often becomes a target of such unjustified response. Therefore, a teacher who intends to work by rational principles must be warned that he is likely to be confronted with a number of arguments against the practice of being clear about what he intends to do. My way of warning is to present a restatement of the more familiar of these arguments and some brief refutations.

One typical argument against the explicit statement of objectives is that some content, particularly literature, possesses such properties that the purposes for teaching it are not accessible to explicit statement, that the objectives are, therefore, "intangible." Replying to that position, I would suggest that the typical teacher of poetry selects poems to read, asks questions, prepares examinations, and the rest. Presumably, this teacher must have in mind some desired outcome or set of outcomes because there are no other rational grounds for making these decisions. If he believes that he cannot express the desired achievements in words, then either he has not really clarified in his own mind what he is after or, if he has, he has not yet bothered to put his intention into clear language.

A second objection maintains that poetry, fiction, or some other kind of content automatically implies the objectives for teaching it and, therefore, these need not be stated. But experience shows that there is no general agreement on objectives for teaching such content.

A third objection contends that there are various ways of stating objectives: In effect, the objector says, "Yes, I do have objectives, but I don't state them in the form that you describe." Here the important point is to state objectives as simply and clearly as possible. I have suggested one procedure. If better ones are available, these should be used.

A fourth objection asserts that the "good teacher" typically does not think of changes to be brought about in learners, but rather thinks of things for students to do in which they will become involved. Such a teacher hopes that valuable outcomes will emerge from involving students in interesting activity. This contention, however, exemplifies a confusion of ends and means. To lose sight of the objective and to confuse it with the means to achieve it creates the kind of confusion that this book is trying to help the teacher avoid. It is probably true that some teachers who confuse ends and means achieve desirable results. But such success neither depends upon, nor justifies, the maintaining of that confusion.

A fifth objection holds that the statement of objectives as changes sought in students inhibits creativity. I would respond that not only do such objectives identify, clarify, and communicate the intent of instruction, they also establish a proper basis for the imaginative selection of activities. A search for and justification of new and unfamiliar objectives is also an exercise in the use of imagination. Clarity of purpose, then, doesn't inhibit the imagination; rather, it clarifies what it is that we are to be imaginative about and what purpose this imaginative and creative activity is to serve.

A sixth objection asserts that the important outcomes of teaching may not be known until many years after the student has left school; it is therefore futile, in this view, to state objectives before or during a unit of instruction. Dewey, however, explains why a wise selection of objectives implies lasting value:

With the advent of democracy and modern industrial conditions, it is impossible to foretell definitely just what civilization will be twenty years from now. Hence it is impossible to prepare the child for any precise set of conditions. To prepare him for the future life means to give him command of himself; it means so to train him that he will have the full and ready use of all his capabilities; that his eye and ear and hand may be tools ready to command, that his judgment may be capable of grasping the conditions under which it has to work, and the executive forces be trained to act economically and efficiently.[7]

In this statement, Dewey suggests a basis for selecting objectives that are permanently valuable.

Finally, a seventh argument maintains that the practice of formulating clear objectives has the effect of limiting instruction to what can be conveniently stated. What can be conveniently stated, the argument goes, are such low-level achievements as capitalization, punctuation, and memorization of the "plots" of stories. My reply is that the trivialization of learning cannot be a consequence merely of the principle and practice of stating objectives; it is rather a consequence of the trivial objectives one has consciously or unconsciously formulated. In a sense, all teachers, despite what they may say, formulate objectives, whether overtly or unconsciously, vaguely or lucidly. But important learning is more likely to be achieved when the conception of that learning is explicitly formulated.

Objectives stated with the degree of precision appropriate to its subject, then, are the proper criteria for deciding on all other aspects of teaching: the selection and organization of learning activities and procedures of evaluation. Yet much work in our schools is misguided by misconceptions, vague conceptions, and confusions about the very purposes for which schools exist. The reader of this book is more likely to meet confusion in his school than clarity. I have identified some of these degradations so that the reader may deal more intelligently with the situation in which he finds himself. Further, I have identified some of the hostility that all too often confronts the teacher of English who tries to work from rational principles.

Selecting and justifying objectives

A community or larger society, in order to survive and to change in desired directions, needs members who possess certain kinds of knowledge, understanding, attitudes, and skills. A member of that society needs certain kinds of learning in order to participate in its affairs, to realize his potential as an individual, and to help his society survive and change. His needs and the needs of society are the sources of educational objectives. The needs, however, are not themselves objectives. For example, if a free and literate society is to maintain itself, its citizens need to think critically. Thus, "Ability to criticize what is read" is a broad goal of education, Level 1 or 2; a related Level 3 objective might be "Identify techniques of persuasion in editorials."

As noted, objectives may be justified by needs of individuals. Suppose that a student has developed an interest in poetry and has become sensitive to its effects. His teacher has encouraged him to become curious about what these effects are and what causes them. From this student's need, we may infer among other possibilities the objective "Explain how lyric poems affect readers." Although attaining this objective may or may not be necessary for the maintenance of society, we may assume, nevertheless, that the purpose of our society is the self-realization of its members. Thus, the meeting of individual needs for self-fulfillment is consistent with what we take the aim of our society to be.

But not all desired achievements are proper to school learning. As an institution possessing distinctive traits and having limited time and resources at its disposal, the school is suited only for certain kinds of instructional tasks. In a study of what the instructional tasks of schools should be, Ralph W. Tyler arrived at this conclusion:

> Tasks of instruction proper to the school in contrast to those proper to other educational agencies (e.g., home, church, scouting) are those requiring:
> (1) *A well-educated faculty.*
> (2) *Well-organized learning activities over extended periods of time.*

Learning the structure of the English language, for example, requires such conditions.

(3) *The kind of learning in which important aspects are not obvious to everyday observation, but must in some way be brought to the student's attention.*

The means through which works of poetry, drama, and fiction achieve their effects are not obvious to typical readers and audiences. Inquiry into literary and dramatic devices, therefore, requires conditions that schools can provide.

(4) *The kind of learning that involves vicarious experiences.*

The everyday life of the typical citizen does not inform him of the long ago and the far away. But the school offers opportunities for such learning. The study of literature is one example.

(5) *The kind of learning in which the content is typically not part of everyday living.*

The following kinds of content are appropriate to the English class, but usually not part of life in the marketplace: the better works of drama, fiction, poetry, linguistic inquiry, and expository writing. Such content implies learning about high standards of judgment and modes of analysis.

(6) *The kind of learning in which activities of everyday living are examined and interpreted.*

In everyday life people are concerned with such matters as goodness, fairness and decency. But conditions of one's daily life are not conducive to his examining and clarifying his conceptions and attitudes toward those matters. The conditions of the school, however, are suited to this kind of reflection and clarification. In the English class, these concerns are appropriate to instruction in composition, group discussion, and serious works of literature.[8]

The preceding discussion implies that an objective is justified if it fulfills a social and individual need and implies the kind of instruction that is properly the concern of the school and of the field of English, however this field may be defined.

Plans and evaluation

It should be clear that if a teacher can derive and state objectives well, his job of selecting materials, scheduling activities, and assisting the progress of his students becomes an intellectually coherent task. In the discussion that follows, we consider this principle as it relates to plans, activities, and evaluation.

Students acquire desired learning by practicing it. If the objective refers to the effects of a poem, the practice must be aimed at identifying those effects. Because the inferring of effects depends on comprehension a class may be asked, for example, to answer such a question as "What is the actual situation in the first four lines of this poem?"

The responses of students to such questions are examples of learning activities. No learning activity is itself good or bad: because it is a means, not an end, a learning activity can be judged good, bad, or indifferent only with reference to the objectives which it serves. The same criteria apply also to teaching and to all other aspects of instruction—tests, materials, and methods.

A *learning activity*, in other words, is what a student does. He may, for example, read a short story, write a paragraph, listen to an explanation, discuss a novel, interview the manager of the local supermarket. From activities, experiences arise.

An *experience* is the result of the student's response to an activity or to his environment in general. It is important to distinguish learning activity from experience. As noted, learning activity refers to what the student does, which necessarily produces in him a reaction or response. As a result of his responses, the student acquires feelings, attitudes, and kinds of understanding or misunderstanding, and increases or decreases in skill. Put another way, it is only through experience, as we have defined that term, that students learn. Objectives are desired experiences.

A desired experience, however, is not a necessary result of a particular learning activity or of a set of these. Two students working at the same activity—for example, reading Act I of *Julius Caesar*—may have quite different experiences, one student being fascinated and the other bored. A constant task of teaching is the selection of learning activities that are likely to produce desired experiences and, therefore, desired achievements. It is in the nature of things that teachers cannot prescribe experiences; they prescribe activities.

Not only are objectives the proper criteria for selecting the materials and procedures of teaching; they are criteria, also, for selecting and devising procedures of evaluation. Evaluating a program of instruction is no different from evaluating any purposeful enterprise: to evaluate is to determine the extent to which the enterprise has achieved its purposes.

By definition, objectives specify purposes of teaching. Therefore, a valid test or other evaluative situation is essentially a translation of the objectives into tasks. How well the learner executes the tasks enables us to determine the extent to which he has acquired the desired learning.

Thus, for the objective "State the literal sense of what is going on in lyric poetry," the following situation may be justified as valid: "Here is a copy of a lyric poem you haven't seen before and that is presumably within your range of comprehension. State the literal sense of what is going on in that poem." (Chapter 3 discusses evaluation further.)

The foregoing discussion suggests that if Level 3 or 4 objectives are carefully stated for a given poem, play, story, or essay, these provide criteria for devising and organizing learning activities and procedures of evaluation.

Finally, the work of the class is psychologically theirs if students not only are aware of the objectives as the teacher has phrased them, but are also provided opportunity to discuss, question, and possibly change some of the objectives.

A method of thinking

To this point, our discussion has implied a method whereby a teacher may conceive and carry out his task. Although the method is necessarily flexible, it is coherent in that it adheres to the principle that teaching is a process of conceiving and justifying objectives, planning and conducting the necessary instruction, and evaluating the achievement of students and, thereby, the success of the program. The discussion has presented some terms and distinctions for carrying out the necessary thinking, planning, and teaching.

This method or procedure may be illustrated as follows: A teacher may begin by accepting one or more objectives at Levels 1 or 2—for example, such a Level 1 objective as "critical thinking." He then may ask himself, "How can the content within English help my students think critically?" Among the kinds of content that schools deem proper to English are newspaper editorials. Knowing that editorials are obviously appropriate materials for critical thinking, and proper to the work of the school, the teacher then may ask, "How can I formulate an intelligible plan of instruction for helping my students learn to respond critically to editorials?" As a student of prose and rhetoric, the teacher knows that critical responses imply an ability to get the literal sense of what is read, to infer its intended effects upon readers, and to make judgments about these. Such abilities, then, would suggest objectives. His experience with his students enables him to decide whether his students are likely to profit from instruction aimed at all or at just some of these.

Let us assume that he believes his students will profit from teaching aimed at all. He would then formulate the Level 3 objectives, select or devise and organize a set of learning activities, and evaluate the extent to which his students have acquired the desired learning. The evaluation would also determine strengths and weaknesses of his instruction. Results of his evaluation would provide a basis for improving his program—for clarifying his objectives, deleting or adding objectives, revising the learning activities and the organization of these, and revising his procedures of evaluation. With changes made, the revised program would be carried out, evaluated, and revised again. In this view, teaching is a cyclical process of planning, trial, evaluation, revision, retrial, and so on without end.

The procedure need not begin with Levels 1 or 2. Perhaps a teacher feels that there is good reason for his class to read

The Price by Arthur Miller. He may then look to Levels 1 or 2 for justification, formulate his Level 3 and 4 objectives, and carry out the rest of the process.

Indeed, a teacher may begin at any point—with a learning activity such as a question or problem with which his students are likely to be concerned, with a Level 3 objective, with an evaluative exercise that he believes his students ought to be able to do, or with an objective at any of the four levels. But in planning a justified and intelligible unit of instruction, the entire process described must in some fashion be fulfilled.

The capabilities of teaching

The foregoing discussion suggests that the ability to teach English or any subject, in any community, in any style or mode of schooling, at any level, may be expressed as a set of seven interrelated skills or capabilities. These skills, shown in the accompanying table, have been inferred from the assumption (or truism) that teaching is a process, both exacting and rational, for imparting desired learning.

Not only are these the capabilities of teaching, they may be viewed also as the principles of teaching defined operationally. Because this list of operational principles hangs together as a unified whole that explicates the competencies of teaching, it provides a rational basis for all classroom decisions.

The wise use of the school's time

In discussing planning and teaching, I have been emphasizing the following kind of procedure: given this objective, it is suitable to propose these learning activities in this order with those evaluative items. Although convenient for explaining the principles of teaching, this procedure does not explain how to make optimal use of the school's time. The fullest use of the school's time implies the fullest use of learning activities. Learning activities are used fully when they are means to a number of objectives. As an example, the reading

CAPABILITIES OF TEACHING

1. Infer and justify what the content of instruction ought to contribute to the education of his students.
2. Translate those potential contributions into statements or some formulation of instructional objectives.
3. Select or devise classroom work or other activities that are likely to develop the learning specified by the objectives.
4. Plan a sequence in which the learning activities are to occur, the sequence being justified by feasibility in achieving the objectives.
5. Evaluate the extent to which the students have acquired the desired learning, a procedure which serves also to evaluate the program of instruction.
6. Conduct the program of instruction and of evaluation implied by all the above.
7. Propose plans, justified by the results of evaluation, for improving the instructional program.

of "A & P" by John Updike may serve objectives (expressed here at Level 2) concerning the comprehension of fiction, the identification of values that are built into literary selections, and an understanding of conditions under which people work.

Justifying learning activities

The section just presented together with the earlier one treating "activity" and "experience" implies criteria for selecting or devising learning activities. Thus, an activity is justified if it is likely to result in the following: (1) practice of behavior specified or implied by the objectives, (2) practice that the student finds interesting (everyone avoids the distasteful and the dull), and (3) practice that serves a number of objectives.

Clarifying a distinction

It is important to distinguish criteria for justifying learning activities from criteria for justifying objectives. For whatever reason, students of teaching have trouble keeping the difference straight. I shall, therefore, repeat the criteria by which objectives are justified. That makes it convenient for the reader to compare these criteria with the three cited in the preceding section. The comparison may help clarify the distinction.

An objective is justified, then, if it can be shown to (1) fulfill a social and individual need and (2) imply the kind of instruction that is properly the concern of the school and of the field of English, however that field may be defined.

These two sets of criteria and the distinction between them are important because they explicate the rational basis for planning classroom work.

Pitfalls

Ideally, the principles of teaching are means to purposeful and intellectually liberating professional practice. In their degradations, the principles are so misconceived and misused that teaching becomes a form of drudgery, slavishness, and intellectual desuetude. Certain practices illustrate some of these distortions. One such practice in planning and teaching is lack of coherent relationships among objectives, learning activities, and evaluation. A second, already discussed, is resistance to the principle of being clear about objectives. A third is excessive specificity in formulating objectives: for example, the stating of some 346 objectives for ninth-grade English, a kind of excess that so enmeshes teacher and student in behavioral detail that the very purpose for stating objectives is defeated.

A fourth is the practice of buying and selling objectives developed in other places, by other teachers, through a process of discussion in which the buyers have not participated. Such a practice disregards the principle that objectives psychologically belong to those who have developed them. When objectives are merely bought, the buyers are not likely to understand or feel psychologically committed to them.

A fifth degradation is the use of rigid checklists. When the construction of a checklist is based on a stereotype of what teaching is supposed to look like, the use of the checklist becomes an unjustified form of repression.

Another unfortunate consequence is the practice of substituting items on a checklist for critical observation based on the principles of teaching. When a teacher is rewarded for conformity to a stereotype or to mere traditional expectation, he is encouraged to become a functionary rather than an independent professional.

Not only is the checklist used as a device for urging conformity, but so are rigid lesson plans. A sixth degrading practice, then, is the attempt to cover a lesson plan rather than adapt teaching to its purpose as well as to the exigencies and interests of the moment.

Finally, a seventh debasement is a result of a teacher's being overwhelmed by what he sees as the vast number of his students' educational needs. His response is to conceive his goals in such broad and vague terms that they suggest the meeting of all the needs. He sees his task as the teaching of reading, writing, good citizenship, and appreciation of the good, the true, and the beautiful. But the realities of teaching suggest that these admirable intentions are most likely to be achieved through instruction determined by a series of carefully selected and formulated Level 3 objectives.

Summary

Conditions necessary for responsible teaching are these:

1. *A set of objectives.* These must be phrased so that one can know what students are able to do as a result of instruction. I have labeled such objectives Level 3. Objectives are justified on grounds that they meet social and individual needs, imply tasks proper to the school and to whatever the content of English may be taken to be. Level 4 objectives are examples of Level 3.

A formulation of objectives that is explicit and useful must specify both behavior and content. The objective "Describe the aspect of human experience depicted in novels" specifies "describe" as the behavior desired; the rest of the statement identifies the content.

Teaching implies the use of particular novels and particular examples of any other content that may be studied. Objectives for actual teaching may be called "Level 4 objectives"; an example is "Describe the aspect of human experience depicted in *The Great Gatsby.*" The real objective, however, is Level 3; Level 4 is a means.

The distinction between Level 3 and Level 4 makes it convenient to adapt examples of content to differing interests and backgrounds. For some classes, *The Great Gatsby* is too sophisticated for teaching the comprehension of fiction. *Old Yeller* by Frank Gipson may be a better choice.

2. *A set of ordered learning activities.* To acquire the desired achievements, the student must be put to work practicing the learning that the objectives specify or imply. The objectives provide criteria for selecting or devising activities. In other words, the selection of learning activities is justified by their use in achieving the objectives, as is the order in which the activities are to occur.

3. *A set of evaluative situations.* To assess the learning

activities, the feasibility of the objectives, and the achievement of students, the program must provide situations in which the student displays the extent to which he has acquired the learning desired. Evaluation is a process of determining the extent to which the learning of students conforms to the learning that the objectives specify. Data from the process of evaluation provide the rational basis for revising programs and improving instruction.

Exercises

Exercise 1

Explain why such words as the following are not useful in stating Level 3 or 4 or instructional objectives: *understand, realize, be aware of, know, gain insight into, see the importance of, have a profound understanding of, improve, learn, study.*

Exercise 2

Comment on the following statement: "When I teach, I don't worry about objectives. Whenever I teach a poem, I just get up there and tell 'em all I know about it."

Exercise 3

A list of Level 2 objectives appears below. Translate each into a Level 3 objective. Students need to:

Know how to use an index to a book.
Understand the difference between statements of fact and statements of opinion.
Be aware of how writers of advertisements attempt to persuade readers.
Learn that different magazines appeal to different social levels of society.
Study mass media.

Exercise 4

For each objective you have formulated for Exercise 3, state a Level 4 objective and relate to it the first learning activity you would devise. Justify your statements.

Exercise 5

Assume that each item on the following list implies a task of instruction. Is each a task appropriate to the school? Give reasons for your replies.

Reading newspapers.

Writing poetry.

Reading highway signs.

Appreciating film.

Understanding television drama.

Exercise 6

From casual observation of the community or larger society in which you live, identify the following, *each to be related to the other.*

A need which you believe English can fill.

Level 2 objective.

Level 3 objective.

Level 4 objective.

A learning activity.

Here is an example:

Need: Our nation, having a free electorate and free and promiscuous media of communication, needs citizens who will not believe everything they hear and read.

Level 2 objective: Read and listen critically.

Level 3 and 4 objectives: Identify techniques of persuasion in political speeches (. . . in Candidate X's speech to be delivered over television tonight).

Learning activity: Listen to Candidate X's speech and be prepared to explain what he tried to get his audience to do or to believe and to identify the techniques he had used as means to his purposes.

Exercise 7

Explain how the teaching of English may become "relevant" to a group of today's secondary school students with whom you have some familiarity. Follow these steps:

a. Explain your view of "relevance" in the teaching of English. State your view in terms of Level 3 objectives and related learning activities. Justify these. Contrast your idea of "relevance" with Level 3 objectives and learning activities that you deem "irrelevant." Explain that "irrelevance."

b. For a Level 1 or 2 objective that you deem relevant, identify a Level 3 and 4 objective, and a learning activity. Justify these latter decisions by reference to your view of relevance and to the section of Chapter 1 that states the criteria for selecting and justifying objectives.

Exercise 8

Explain why *in and of themselves* there can be no such thing as good learning activities, good materials, or good teaching.

Notes

1. This chapter explains a method by which teachers and other educators may inquire into problems of planning and teaching. The general "conceptual framework" is taken from Ralph W. Tyler's booklet, *Basic Principles of Curriculum and Instruction* (Chicago: University of Chicago Press, 1950).

2. The notion of four levels of objectives is taken from J. N. Hook, "The Tri-University BOE Project: A Progress Report," in *On Writing Behavioral Objectives for English*, ed. John Maxwell and Anthony Tovatt (Champaign, Ill.: Commission on the English Curriculum of the National Council of Teachers of English, 1970), pp. 75–86.

3. Paul Woodring, *A Fourth of a Nation* (New York: McGraw-Hill, 1957), p. 111.

4. Alfred North Whitehead, *The Aims of Education and Other Essays* (Mentor Books; New York: New American Library of World Literature, 1949), p. 11.

5. National Education Association, Educational Policies Commission, *The Central Purpose of American Education* (Washington, D.C.: The Association, 1961), p. 12.

6. John Dewey, *The Sources of a Science of Education* (New York: Horace Liveright, 1929), pp. 12–13.

7. John Dewey, "My Pedagogic Creed" (1897), reprinted in

An American Primer, ed. Daniel J. Boorstin (Mentor Books; New York: New American Library, 1966), p. 633.

8. Tyler's criteria for selecting tasks appropriate to the school appear, among other places, in his article "New Criteria for Curriculum Content and Method," in *The High School in a New Era,* ed. Francis Chase and Harold A. Anderson (Chicago: University of Chicago Press, 1958), pp. 173–76.

CHAPTER 2

THE COMPREHENSION OF EXPOSITION AND ARGUMENT: LITERAL SENSE AND PART-WHOLE

A piece of exposition or argument says something literally and produces effects upon audiences. These two properties imply skills of comprehension and activities for learning.

Properties of exposition and argument

A piece of exposition or argument possesses many properties. It says something literally; it persuades or informs readers and audiences; it exemplifies a process of reasoning. In addition, it is an index of the writer's mind and vision; it reflects a particular time and circumstance; it may convey and explain social, political, moral, and religious values. And so on.

Each of these properties implies skills of comprehension or ideas from which to draw inferences. Because an argument says something literally, we may comprehend it for its literal sense. Because an argument persuades, we may comprehend it as an example of rhetoric. And so it goes for the other properties that exposition and argument possess.

In this book I limit the treatment of comprehension to the first three properties on our list: literal sense; rhetoric, communication, or "part-whole" analysis; and reasoning or "analysis of ideas." This chapter treats the first two properties and Chapter 4 treats the third. The three kinds of comprehension are prerequisite to the drawing of social, moral, psychological, and other inferences and, moreover, provide a foundation for teaching and learning to write exposition and argument, the subject of Chapter 5.

Literal-sense comprehension

The recovery of the literal sense is fundamental to all learning that requires the use of any kind of connected discourse. Elementary and high-school students have difficulty getting the literal sense as do graduate students, their professors, and writers of books, articles, and letters to the editor. This contention is amply sustained by the experiences of students, teachers, and those who read controversies among authors and their critics, particularly in the many instances in which an author claims that his critic hasn't understood the literal sense of what he has written.

To improve the student's use of this skill, begin by selecting a brief expository passage that has a unity of its own and that students find interesting. Then lead a discussion based upon this question: "In one sentence, what, mainly, is the writer saying?" The discussion will be profitable only when students are required to justify their replies by explicit reference to the text. This practice of verification is fundamental to the responsible comprehension and discussion of any piece of writing.

The following passage exemplifies those that may be used with students who are average or above; it was written by the assistant managing editor of *The New York Times*:

> Thirty years ago it was not uncommon for our editors to refuse to print an explanation of, say, a bill in Congress on the ground that "we printed that only six months ago," as if readers maintained a running index of newspaper articles and kept referring to it day by day. Or editors would not define an obscure term because it could be found in the dictionary, as if every commuter train had a Webster's Unabridged installed right opposite the men's room. Or they would not take the space to explain the Malthusian law since "any high school senior knows that." Which was true enough, except that a

goodly segment of their readers had not been high school seniors for ten or fifty years, and another segment had not yet reached that station.

Today we think it well to make each issue as nearly self-sufficing as is reasonable, so that the reader does not feel the need for a research staff to help him understand the day's news. Perhaps the best slogan a newspaper could post in its city room would be this: "Keep two readers always in mind: the high school sophomore and the man who has been marooned on a desert island for three months." Both of them, for different reasons, have to be told what it is all about.[1]

In teaching this passage or anything else, it is useful to realize that there are no rules of teaching and no sacrosanct lists of activities. There is, however, a set of necessary and invariant principles through which the teacher leads his students to desired achievements. A formulation of the principles appears in the section "The Capabilities of Teaching" in Chapter 1. The principles free a teacher to choose or devise whatever means he wishes for achieving his goal.

Here the goal is restated by the question noted above. The procedures described for reaching this goal and others will often be couched in the imperative, which I use for brevity of statement and ease of reading. The examples of procedures, however expressed, are illustrations of the use of principles; they are not prescriptions.

If a passage to be read does not appear in the students' text or other material, it may be presented by duplicated handout, overhead projection, or writing on the board. Before asking them to read, anticipate difficulties they may have with vocabulary or with ideas that the text presents. Resolve these difficulties as simply and directly as possible. Don't send them to reference books. Keep the activity moving. One plan is to list the anticipated difficulties on the board and supply the explanations briefly. For the passage at hand, the following items may be listed and their meanings explained: *not uncommon, Malthusian law, self-sufficing, segment.*

If students are to know what a discourse says they must

be supplied, somehow or other, with the meanings of vocabulary, allusions, or references that they don't know. The reason for this may seem strange at first: Readers don't get meaning from the page; rather, they bring meaning to the page. Consider, for example, the two following words: *dog* and *aligbate*. Although a reader may have no trouble with *dog*, he probably doesn't know what *aligbate* means and therefore can't read it. If he had experience with *aligbate*, then reading it would present no problem. It is misleading, therefore, to suppose that a reader gets meaning out of a page; it is more accurate to say that reading is a process of bringing meaning to the page. If, therefore, students lack some of the experience that the page requires, it must be supplied. (For the curious, *aligbate* is a Philippine vegetable that resembles a combination of spinach and okra.) Discourses that mainly call for experiences quite beyond those that the reader has are too difficult.

Having explained the hard words in the passage at hand, ask the students to read it straight through fairly rapidly and then to be prepared to explain in one sentence what it is mainly saying. Tell them to be able to justify their answers by referring to the particularities of the passage.

To the question of what, mainly, the passage is saying the typical replies fall into four classes: the student misses the point completely; he overgeneralizes by giving some such reply that the passage above is about writing; he takes a subordinate aspect for the whole and may say that the passage is about a bill in Congress, or the Malthusian law, or being marooned on a desert island; or he gives an acceptable answer.

What should be done for the student who misses the point completely? He should be encouraged to listen to the discussion, ask questions, and contribute whatever he can. Those who make the two other kinds of mistakes should be led to reexamine the passage. For the student who overgeneralizes, ask him some such question as this: "What kind of writing does the author refer to? Short stories? Novels? Justify your reply." For the student who mistakes a minor aspect for the main point, ask something like this: "Why does the author use the phrases, 'a bill in Congress,' 'Malthusian law,' 'marooned on a desert island'? In other words, explain the work these phrases do within the passage."

The student who gets things right should be expected to contribute more to the discussion and to read more difficult selections.

I can think of no better means for developing skill in comprehension than the give and take of class discussion. In developing comprehension, use materials related to whatever concerns students have or may be encouraged to have. Teachers can adapt topics and levels of difficulty to particular groups because of the abundance of published materials available and accessible in newspapers, magazines, and books.

A warning must be issued against the practice of trying to teach comprehension simply by presenting students with passages and questions on it for them to answer in writing. If they could do such exercises without having been taught, then they don't need to be taught because they already know. Written exercise, therefore, should be viewed as practice of achievements that have been previously taught. We must distinguish, therefore, instruction from practice.

There can be no cut and dried procedure for teaching all selections. Each selection has its own problems, and each learner his own difficulties. But inferring needs for teaching and asking appropriate questions are useful not only for teaching expository prose, but also for teaching students to get the literal sense of other forms of writing.

To clarify this view of teaching for literal sense, I cite another passage and illustrate the ideas just presented.

I decline to accept the end of man. It is easy enough to say that man is immortal simply because he will endure: that when the last ding-dong of doom has clanged and faded from the last worthless rock hanging tideless in the last red and dying evening, that even then there will still be one more sound: that of his puny inexhaustible voice, still talking. I refuse to accept this. I believe that man will not merely endure: he will prevail. He is immortal, not because he alone among creatures has an inexhaustible voice, but because he has a soul, a spirit capable of compassion and sacrifice and endurance. The poet's, the writer's duty is to write about these things. It is his privilege to help man endure by lifting his heart, by reminding him of the courage and honor and hope and pride and compassion and pity and sacrifice which have been the glory of his past. The poet's voice need not merely be the record of man, it can be one of the props, the pillars to help him endure and prevail.[2]

Ask the students to explain in one sentence what the writer is mainly saying. Following is a desirable answer and justification for it: "Not only is the job of the writer to write about man's soul and spirit, but also to help him prevail." The author begins with the assertion that man will not come to an end (first three sentences) but that he will prevail because he has a soul and spirit "capable of compassion and sacrifice and endurance" (fourth sentence). The last three sentences discuss the "writer's duty." Here the author asserts that the duty of the writer is not only to record man's courage, honor, pride, and compassion but also to help him endure and prevail.

Part-whole comprehension[3]

Literal-sense comprehension may be viewed as a specific aim of instruction or as part of a larger view of comprehension which we may call "part-whole." Part-whole comprehension begins with the assumption that a piece of writing is an example of communication. The purpose of communication is to produce effects upon audiences and readers. It follows that the purpose of a communicative discourse is not to express ideas and not to say something. Rather, what may be expressed, described, or argued is a means to the producing of effects. For the prose of exposition and argument, the typical effects are to inform the reader or to persuade him. A piece of writing may seek any combination of these effects and others. The number of effects possible is the number of effects that language can produce.

To clarify, I restate the ancient truth that the first principle of any activity or object is its purpose. For a Chevrolet, transportation is its purpose and first principle of construction. Therefore, the form of the car, the manufacturing process, and the kinds of materials it is made out of are determined by the necessity to provide transportation. Because the first principle of an argument, viewed as communication, is to produce certain effects upon intended readers, a properly written discourse is so constructed that it can be defended as a means for achieving those effects.

It is important to guard against the notion that the effects must in fact be achieved. Not only is universal attainment of rhetorical purpose impossible, and undesirable if it were possible, but "an art is not properly evaluated by its effects but by its principles."[4] An argument explaining this appears in the section "Evaluation of the student teacher" in Chapter 3. Meanwhile, only a moment's reflection shows why the effects of arguments cannot and should not always be achieved. Well-written discourse can urge support of the American Nazi Party as well as support of the most praiseworthy of causes.

To think clearly about purpose, it is useful to realize that the purpose of a thing is never a part of the thing. Transportation, the purpose of a Chevrolet, is not part of it. A perfectly good Chevrolet can exist even though it is not providing transportation. Similarly, an ax exists as a completed whole whether or not it is actually cutting through wood.

Like a car or an ax, a discourse is a made thing whose purpose is not part of it. A piece of exposition may explain how to buy a used car. But its purpose, an informed reader, is necessarily not part of the discourse. Even if it does not actually inform, the discourse exists as a whole and concrete entity. But purpose determines what it is and what it consists of. A composition viewed as communication is a made thing that is determined by its desired effects.

The ideas just discussed, though fundamental, may be unfamiliar. To help readers and their prospective students comprehend these ideas more fully, I present the following set of exercises.

Exercises

Exercise 1

For some purposeful object, draw distinctions between the object itself and its purpose. For example, consider a chair, a telephone, a pen. Relate the discussion to a piece of writing such as a news report. Make clear why the purpose of a piece of writing viewed as communication is not a part of the discourse.

Exercise 2

Explain why "to inform" implies a purpose but "to explain" implies a means. Draw similar distinctions between "to enlighten" and "to justify," "to astonish" and "to differentiate," "to amuse" and "to describe."

Exercise 3

A writer may begin with the sentence, "The purpose of this article is to explain the causes of air pollution in Chicago." Although that sentence may be suitable, in a sense it is misleading. Why?

Exercise 4

Explain how the purpose of a piece of expository prose may change even though its subject remains the same. Take as an example any subject: the neighborhood pharmacy, a familiar local industry, or whatever. How may the same subject be used in one essay to inform, in another to persuade, and in another to entertain?

Exercise 5

It is common to hear a chairman say that the speaker "needs no introduction." Assume this to be true. In other words, assume that the audience does indeed know the speaker, his background, and his accomplishments. Assume, too, that the introduction supplies the audience with no new information and that the occasion calls for no efforts to persuade. What, then, would be the purpose of the introduction? In your reply, be on guard against confusing ends and means.

Examples of the confusion would be revealed by such phrases as "to explain . . . ," "to share with the audience. . . ." State the purpose as effects to be produced upon the audience. Do not state the purpose as what the writer is to do or as what the discourse is to say.

Exercise 6

The distinction drawn between the ends and means of a piece of writing is typically not a matter of one's consciously organized knowledge. Write a brief exposition intended to inform a seventh-grader of this distinction.

Part-whole skills for comprehending exposition and argument

Having explained the ends and means of a piece of expository prose, I shall discuss the parts or causes incorporated into the discourse by which the effects are produced. We shall see that these parts consist of a single set for all examples of such prose and that it implies skills of comprehension.

If a reader is to be informed by means of words, the verbal discourse must consist of an explanation. If he is to be persuaded, the discourse must be an argument. I call such an explanation or argument a "whole." Such a whole is necessarily made available to the reader through its author, who consciously or unconsciously does certain things that result in particular causes of effects. I call these causes "parts." These unavoidable and necessary parts derive from the author's representing himself as a certain kind of person; conveying certain attitudes toward himself, his topic, and his audience; and selecting, organizing, and emphasizing whatever details or other information he presents. I call these "nonverbal parts." The author, moreover, selects the words, which are the material that verbal discourses are made of. I call the language the "verbal part." These parts are not evaluative terms; they are conditions of a work's existence.

To this point, our discussion of part-whole comprehension is conceptualized in the accompanying table as a set of skills that define part-whole comprehension.

PART-WHOLE SKILLS FOR COMPREHENDING EXPOSITION AND ARGUMENT

1. *Purpose:* Identify each of the following and justify and confirm that decision by explicit reference to the text:
   1.1. Intended effects.
   1.2. Perceived reader(s).
2. *Form or the whole:* Identify the main explanation or argument. (If the purpose is to persuade that skill in typing ought to be required for high-school graduation, the main argument must be "skill in typing ought to be required for high-school graduation.")
3. *Nonverbal parts:* Apart from language, the nonverbal parts are the constituents of the whole. Identify each part, justify and confirm that decision by explicit reference to the text, and explain how each part functions to produce the intended effects. As a result of inquiring into parts 3.1–3.5, the audience should be able to explain what is presented (3.3), in what order (3.4), to what extent (3.5), and in what light (3.1, 3.2). In applying this set of skills, relate each part to the whole or to the effects. Following is a list of the parts:
   3.1. The kind of person the selection represents the author as being, or the personal characteristics of the writer as represented by the piece of writing.
   3.2. The attitude he conveys toward himself, his topic, or his audience. (Usually only one of these attitudes is dominant. Account only for the one dominant attitude.)
   3.3. The details: facts, opinions, data, or whatever.
   3.4. The order in which the details are presented.
   3.5. The emphasis.

Distinguishing the personal characteristics of the writer (3.1) from the attitudes he conveys (3.2)

This distinction, in particular, proves vexing. Further clarification, therefore, is needed.

The phrase, "personal characteristics of the writer," refers to the kind of person the piece of writing represents the writer as being. It may or may not mean the kind of person the writer "really" is. Obviously, the personal characteristics of the author as these are represented must be a rhetorical device of some force. We trust people we perceive as wise and we distrust people we perceive as foolish.

"Attitude" (3.2) refers to the author's emotions or feelings toward something, someone, or some group. When in the *Rhetoric* Aristotle discusses the character of the orator, he shows that audiences trust speakers when they take them to possess three traits: I would classify two of these, good morals and prudence or good sense, under personal characteristics (3.1). I would classify the third, good will toward the audience, under attitude (3.2).

On this issue, James H. Sledd, commenting on an early draft of this book, wrote:

> The term *attitude* has always been vague to me. Some people translate it "disposition to act in a particular way." Since we act to get what we consider good, I'd go on to translate *attitude* as "judgment of what's good or bad; assumed values."

Attitude, in this sense, implies values or what is taken to be important or unimportant, good or bad, valuable or valueless.

This distinction and its uses in comprehension will be examined presently in discussions of particular selections.

Further explanation and example

In the introduction to this book, there is a section called "Underlying theory"; a rereading of it may give a useful background for the discussion that follows. That section explains the sense in which purpose determines everything else about an activity or a made thing.

For the comprehension skills listed above, the skills of purpose (1) refer to the final cause, final in the sense that effects determine, finally, everything about the discourse. The skill of form (2) is analogous to the formal cause because the form made is an argument. The skills of nonverbal parts (3) correspond to the efficient cause, which refers to the work of the maker or writer. What the writer does is construct a set of nonverbal parts and embody these in words.

In other words, the writer constructs the parts from which the reader infers the argument and the intended effects. The reader draws these inferences because the writer's work is guided, consciously or not, by the effects and the form or main argument.

As noted, the words constitute the verbal part. I have omitted these because the reader unavoidably uses the skills of language (or the verbal skills) in performing any other comprehension skill whatsoever. In teaching comprehension, therefore, one teaches whatever language skill a student needs: the meanings of words, the interpretation of figures of speech, and so on. These should be taught as the need arises and not as exercises isolated from real problems of comprehension.

These ideas may be clarified by observing their uses in the part-whole comprehension of the following short argument.

Crime in Depression Years

To the Editor:

In your Oct. 12 editorial "Sharing the Blame" dealing with the alarming rise in criminal arrests in our city, you list the underlying causes for the tremendous increase as pervasive poverty, inadequate employment opportunities, failures in education.

While I do not question this statement, I wonder why in the Great Depression, when these conditions were many times worse than they are today, crime was no major issue.

It seems to me that you are overlooking a number of other major contributing factors.

Fred J. Kulb
New York, Oct. 18, 1970[5]

The effect is to persuade the reader that poverty, unemployment, and unsuccessful schooling do not in themselves account for the increase in New York City's crime. It follows that the main argument may be expressed by the clause in the preceding sentence beginning with "poverty" and extending to the end.

To bring about this effect, the selection represents the author as informed, intelligent, tactful, and concerned. The personal characteristics are his being informed, intelligent, and tactful. Concern is his attitude. He is concerned with the problem of crime in his city. His reading the editorial on crime and then taking the time and trouble to respond are evidence of his concern. We infer that he is well informed by noting the distinction he has drawn between the incidence of crime as it was during the Depression and as it is now. He demonstrates intelligence by uncovering simplemindedness in the editorial to which he refers, and he displays tact with the gentle closing sentence: "It seems to me that you are overlooking a number of other major contributing factors." Tact—with perhaps a touch of sly understatement.

The personal characteristics of the writer and the attitude that the letter represents are those that strike readers as trustworthy. Referring again to Aristotle's triad of good sense, good morals, and good will toward the reader, we have seen how the letter gives the impression of the writer's good morals and intelligence or good sense. His good will toward the reader is suggested by his concern with the problem of crime in their city.

The selection and order of details may be briefly explained: first, a reference to an earlier editorial that the writer finds dubious, and, second, a counterargument to that editorial including a suggestion that the editorial failed to make sense because it omitted "a number of other major contributing factors." Because the writer seeks to persuade by presenting a counterargument, a rational person would expect to find, first, the original argument refuted and the counterargument following. But the writer also suggests why the editorial went wrong, a brief diagnosis that arouses further trust in the writer's perspicuity and, thereby, trust in what he says.

The emphasis is on those details that show the contrast between the rate of crime now and as it was during the Depression. This helps persuade that the social conditions noted in the editorial fail to explain the increase in crime.

The discussion just concluded not only identifies the parts but also the functioning of the parts. When parts are discussed without reference to their function, they are treated not as constituents of a whole but as discrete topics unrelated to reasons for their existence.

Comprehension and inference

The discussion so far has shown that the following aspects of comprehension can be verified from the particularities of the text: what the text literally says, and what the effects, parts, and functionings of parts are. For example, the discussion of the letter on New York City's crime shows that these matters are accessible to verification. Any number of competent readers, then, will reach the same understanding, although they will give it individual expression if asked to explain. But not all competent readers will necessarily agree with the argument, nor will they all place similar value on it.

There is a difference, therefore, between matters of agreement and value with respect to a statement, on the one hand, and the comprehension of it, on the other. I shall call matters of agreement and value "inference" and distinguish it from "comprehension." The distinction needs to be kept straight: A necessary condition for a profitable inquiry into any text is that accurate comprehension be prerequisite to discussions of inference.

Teaching the terms and distinctions

A profitable discussion can occur only when the participants share a common understanding of the topic and the terms related to that topic. The discussion that follows illustrates procedures for developing this common body of understanding.

The assumption behind part-whole comprehension is that

a piece of writing is a thing made to achieve particular effects. A first step in teaching would be to establish that idea. To start, the teacher may say something like this: "In our study of comprehension, we're going to assume that a piece of writing is similar to my Plymouth, which is a thing made for a purpose. In other words, the purpose of my Plymouth is transportation. But is transportation part of my Plymouth?" (No.) "What is the purpose of this chair?" (Sitting.) "Is sitting a part of the chair?" (No.) "What is the purpose of a pen?" (Writing a message.) "Is the written message part of the pen?" (No.) And so forth until the class is led to the conclusion that the purpose of a thing is not part of the thing itself. The conclusion should be explicitly stated and clearly understood.

That knowledge provides background for a learner to explain why a piece of writing may be viewed as a thing whose purpose is not part of that thing. It is useful to start by helping learners see that communication is a process of producing effects upon readers and audiences, that a piece of writing is an example of communication, and that the purpose of a piece of writing, therefore, is not to say something but to produce effects upon readers.

The teacher may continue by baldly asserting that a piece of writing is an example of communication, and then asking: "Suppose I were alone in the middle of the woods and said something. Would I be communicating?" (No.) "Then what does communication mean?" (To say something to someone.) "Yesterday a nuclear physicist was explaining something about his field to me. I didn't understand him. Was he communicating?" (No.) "Now, what would you say communication is?" (Having someone understand what you're saying.) "That seems to be a pretty good idea of what's usually meant by communication. But let's try to be clearer on what we mean by 'understand.' When you listen to Carol Burnett tell a joke, is that joke an example of communication?" (Yes.) "Earlier we saw that the purpose of a thing is not part of the thing. What is the purpose of this thing called a Carol Burnett joke?" (To make people laugh.) "Yes, or to amuse, or to entertain. We may say that if a person understands a good joke, he is entertained. And the joke may be read as well as heard."

"Every morning I read the weather report to find out the weather for the day. What is the purpose of this thing called a weather report?" (To let people know what the weather will be like.) "Yes. We could say that the purpose is to inform."

"For another example, there's a series of articles in the *Times-Union* that tells about smoking pot. What purpose or purposes are those articles intended to serve?" (To let people know about pot.) "Certainly. Anything else?" (To try to discourage people from smoking it.) "Yes. Some purposes are to persuade. We have now arrived at purposes that are usual to pieces of writing. I'll write them on the board:

Some Purposes of What Is Read

To entertain

To inform

To persuade

Are these purposes part of the thing that is read?" (No. They are effects upon readers and not part of the thing read.)

"Obviously, effects don't simply happen all by themselves; they are produced by causes. What causes you to laugh when you hear a Carol Burnett joke?" (The situation she describes.) "Right. When you read a weather report, what causes you to be informed?" (The statements of what the weather is supposed to be.) "Yes. What may persuade you to believe that Woodrow Wilson was a great President?" (An argument showing that he did important things.)

Teaching the basic ideas

"Our discussion reminds us that there are causes of effects. Let me project these on the screen and then we'll discuss how the effects are produced by these causes."

1. The whole or the main explanation or argument.
2. The nonverbal parts that constitute the whole and that make the whole available to the reader.

> 2.1. The kind of person the selection represents its author as being. (Or the personal characteristics of the writer as revealed by the selection.)
> 2.2. The attitude he conveys toward himself, his topic, his audience.
> 2.3. The details, for example, facts, opinions, thoughts, ideas, etc.
> 2.4. The order in which the details are presented.
> 2.5. The emphasis.

"We could say that there are two parts to a hammer, the head and the handle. That means there's at least one sense in which the parts and the whole amount to the same thing. Let us suppose for the moment that on this chart, 1 as well as 2.1 to 2.5 amount to the same thing: 1 represents the whole and 2.1 to 2.5 represent the parts. Are you as the reader most directly presented with 1 or with 2.1 to 2.5? (I'm most directly presented with 2.1 to 2.5 because I have to look at the details and all the rest before I can figure out the whole or what's mainly being said.)

"Yes. When you come right down to it, a piece of writing presents us only with 2.1 to 2.5 and with the words that give us access to all this. We will call 2.1 to 2.5 the nonverbal parts and the words the verbal part. From the nonverbal and verbal parts, we infer the main explanation or argument and the intended effects. Let's get a clearer idea of all this by looking rather closely at a brief piece of writing."

An illustrative passage

"Read this passage that I'm projecting (or that you have in front of you) and tell me what kind of person the author seems to be.

> The constant traffic between classroom and nurse's office can be very trying. Right in the middle of your best pitch for the inversion method of fractional division a hand will go up. Glowing with your prowess as a teacher, eager to answer any and all questions, you call on the frantically

waving paw. "Mr. Hannan," she calls, "kin I go to the
nurse?" Several such incidents may lead you to consider
drastic steps to control the hypochondriac.[6]

Identifying the kind of person the discourse represents the
author as being and the attitude he conveys

"If you'll think about it for a minute, you'll realize that an
argument has to be presented by an author and that he
comes through the piece of writing as being a certain kind of
person. In this passage, tell me what you can about the kind
of person the author, Joseph F. Hannan, presents himself as
being?" (As a conscientious teacher who's interested in
teaching.)

Justifying the response

"Right. How do you know?" (He mentions teaching frac-
tions and glowing with pride about it. Also he tells of being
disappointed with a student who isn't really interested.) "Yes.
Not only do we know that he's a teacher; we know also what
he's interested in teaching."

Identifying purpose or intended effects and
justifying the response

"How shall we relate all this to the purpose of the selection?" (Let's figure out the purpose first, and then do the
relating.) "All right; what is the purpose?" (It's to persuade
the reader that the "constant traffic between classroom and
nurse's office can be very trying." The author says that at the
beginning and then he gives an example to prove it.)

Showing how "representation of author"
functions to produce intended effects

"But how does his being an interested teacher relate to
this purpose?" (We tend to believe people who have firsthand knowledge of what they discuss. And we tend to trust
people who are interested in doing such things as teaching
arithmetic.)

Identifying selection and order of
details and justifying the response

"What information does the author present and in what
order?" (First he states his argument, then describes an incident to back it up, and then makes a kind of nasty comment
on this kind of incident.)

Showing the function of selection and
order in producing effects

"Very fine. Not only have you explained the details but
you've also stated their order. Why this order rather than
some other?" (Because it makes things clear and easy to
understand. Also, the author has decided to affect us by
recounting an incident, which means telling it as it happened.)

Identifying, justifying, and showing function of emphasis

"All right. Can you tell me what in this selection is emphasized and why?" (The author's expression of annoyance is
emphasized. I know this because it runs through the entire
selection, from the first sentence, to the incident, to the
author's nasty crack at the end. He emphasized his annoyance
because that's mainly what he wants to persuade the reader
of.)

Identifying the intended reader and justifying the response

"O.K. Now we've discussed the parts and effects and the
relations between the two. Our discussion isn't complete,
however, because we haven't identified the kind of reader at
whom the selection has apparently been aimed. How would
you describe this reader? (Ordinary, everyday people or the
general public. The language and the topic are probably too
simple for people with lots of education. *Hypochondriac* is
the only hard word.)

Some generalizations

The foregoing imaginary discussion suggests, first, the
feasibility of part-whole comprehension. It suggests, second,

a kind of discussion suited to the skills to be taught. Any passage within the students' range of comprehension and interest is grist for this mill. Conduct as many of these discussions as necessary for the students to develop facility. For independent practice they may be given passages and related questions to which they respond in writing.

Other considerations for discussing a text

To suggest the kind and direction of discussion, I have used an imaginary dialogue of exemplary questions and exemplary replies. Everyone knows, however, that in real life, classroom discussions, expectably, are halting affairs. If they weren't, there would be no need to hold them. A slick and untrammeled discussion that flows without blunder or detour to a defensible conclusion suggests that the students involved already possess the desired achievements.

During the real discussion, students reveal what they need to be taught. They need to be taught whatever is hindering their comprehension. If in discussing a passage, a student doesn't know what "the Dred Scott decision" refers to, although the context clarifies it, direct him to the context and ask him to infer the meaning. If the context doesn't clarify, give a brief explanation and move the discussion along. The discussion should not be held up while the student looks up the Dred Scott decision in a reference source.

A list of comprehension skills guides the teaching of what the students need to know. The needs may include vocabulary, topical references, the comprehension of a particular sentence, and so on. If such explanations take too much time, the selection is probably too hard for the group.

There are no rules, tricks, or gimmicks for holding a discussion. The operational principles of teaching listed earlier in Chapter 1 are the proper guides. This implies that the teacher with the goal and the students in mind gives such explanations and asks such questions that the students will practice the capabilities.

Some prospective teachers worry about communicating with students whose backgrounds differ from theirs. The experience of teaching suggests that the problem is not in communicating; rather, the problem is in finding topics common to student and teacher so that communication that serves instructional ends can occur.

People are genetically endowed with the ability to communicate with others who are different in age and in culture. It is this endowment that enables groups to form interactive communities, including that of the classroom. This is proven by the everyday experience of teachers and others who work successfully with people of differing generations and cultures.

Comprehension for reluctant readers

By reluctant readers, I mean those whom the school finds to be below expectation. A school usually separates the reluctant from others by scores on normed and other reading tests and by the judgments of teachers, supervisors, and guidance counselors. In a typical class of reluctant readers, there are some who are called hyperactive, some who seem apathetic, and others who appear unduly hostile. Teachers of English are often asked to teach classes of such students.

To suggest procedures for teaching such a class, I shall describe those followed in a particular ninth grade of an urban school. The description that follows is based on the assumption that the object is literal-sense comprehension. There was a wide range of ability, and so it was feasible to group. This class was grouped as follows, based on reading scores of a standardized test:

Group 1. 5.5–7.9
Group 2. 3.9–5.4
Group 3. Non-readers

For all groups, the teacher collected back copies of magazines having lots of pictures along with plain, simple words: *Hot Rod, Ebony, Sepia, Scholastic Scope, Black Stars, Jet, Sport,* and *Soul Confessions,* for example. He distributed copies, asked the students to read at leisure, and to exchange, quietly, with others when they had finished with one magazine. Not only was the aim to quiet them down, but also to encourage their getting some satisfaction from the printed page.

To help such a class improve its reading, the teacher must identify those who cannot recognize simple words on sight. The skill of word recognition requires specialized remedial teaching, which a school is obligated to provide. An excellent, uncomplicated diagnostic procedure is oral reading. The teacher took some time to hear each of the less able of the group read a passage of simple prose. Thus, the student revealed whether he could understand the passage. The teacher checked comprehension informally by asking simple questions.

Those who couldn't recognize words, the non-readers, were given special instruction aimed at three objectives: to identify on sight a selection of some seventy-five simple, high frequency words, to associate sound and letter (phonic skill), and to restate ideas in simple selections that consist mainly of words met in the word-recognition activities.

For the non-reader the school invested a few dollars in such materials as these:

Pre-Primer Words Flash Cards, Geller-Widmer Company, St. Louis.
Picture Words For Beginners—For Grades 1 through 3, Milton Bradley Company, Springfield, Mass.
Phonetic Drill Cards—For Grades 1 through 3, Milton Bradley Company, Springfield, Mass.

The first of these are intended to develop a basic sight vocabulary and the third to help with phonic skill. Ideally, a member of the school's reading or guidance staff would handle the job. No such help was available, so the teacher selected a student to work with the students under his direction.

For the two groups of learners who can at least recognize simple words, he developed their comprehension by giving instruction and practice mainly in three skills: inferring the main argument or assertion, inferring ideas that are clearly stated in the text, and inferring ideas that are not clearly stated but that logically follow from what the text says.

Instruction consisted of discussing with them the text they had read and the questions they had responded to.

For example, in such material as McCall-Crabbs *Standard Test Lessons in Reading,* Books A, B, C, and D, (Bureau of Publications, Teachers College, Columbia University) there are multiple choice questions intended to elicit the three kinds of comprehension skill just mentioned.

By discussing their responses, the teacher was instructing them in those skills. The discussion would entail such matters as the reasons why one choice was made for the main explanation or argument and why the other choices were rejected.

In discussing questions on clearly stated details, he asked the students to "prove" their replies by reading the relevant passage of the text aloud.

Instruction in the skill of inferring ideas not specifically stated consisted mainly of discussing replies to questions intended to elicit the use of that skill. For example, if the text described a situation in which bands are playing, lemonade is being sold, and fireworks are going off, the teacher would ask what time of the year it is, and even what day of the year it is.

Another such activity consisted of discussions of items from such a source as *Reading for Understanding* by Thelma Gwinn Thurstone (Science Research Associates). The teacher copied an exercise on the board, including the four choices. Discussion of the passage and the choices was aimed at helping the students determine why only one of the choices was clearly the right one.

Although class discussion involved all students, the distinctions among the groups were used to differentiate materials for individual practice.

Pitfalls

The teaching of comprehension becomes distorted when the skills to be taught are not based upon the needs of learners but on an arbitrary listing that appears in a textbook or teacher's guide. A second corruption is the practice of asking students to identify parts without reference to their functions. In such practice, the parts are treated as separate entities rather than as parts that function within a whole. A third degradation is the practice of tolerating answers that are hunches or undisciplined impressions rather than conclusions that are verifiable from the particularities of the text. Such activity is worse than a waste of time; it is downright mis-educational. Finally, a fourth debasement is any activity entailing a confusion of comprehension with inference, as these terms have been defined. Matters of comprehension are verifiable from the text. An inference, ideally, stems from what has already been comprehended and is a matter of personal values.

Summary

Expository and argumentative prose exhibits, among others, two properties from which skills of comprehension may be inferred. For one thing, such prose is a verbal composition that expresses ideas, and the comprehension of it implies the inferring of its *literal sense*. Second, it is a form of communication that consists of a set of parts for attaining its communicative purpose. We use the term *part-whole* to name the process of comprehending the discourse as communication.

Part-whole comprehension is the more complicated of the two. Not only does it lead to clearer understanding, it also helps to provide a background for expository writing. Some implications of teaching this view of comprehension follow.

1. The skills of part-whole comprehension may be used in varying order. But these constitute a unified set in the sense that all contribute to viewing the work as a means to produce particular effects upon intended readers.

2. The use of the skills results in increased precision and coherence of understanding: This is a result of parts treated as parts, not parts treated as discrete topics.

3. The skills have been inferred from the purpose, the whole, and the verbal and nonverbal parts and stated at a level of generality that is useful for instruction. Within those limits, the list comprises an exhaustive inventory. A teacher's

understanding of the skills gives him a basis for teaching whatever other skills his students need as prerequisite.

4. There is no logical or empirical reason to suppose that the teaching of all skills requires a sequential hierarchy. The same set of skills applies equally to the fourth grader and to the president of IBM. Instruction, therefore, implies selecting differing means for various learners. The skills to be learned are the same for all.

5. Such phrases as "author's purpose" are usually ambiguous. No matter what effects an author may have intended, if the parts of his discourse do not contain the causes for producing the effects, these will neither be achieved nor inferred from his composition. Such intentions are, therefore, useless for comprehending. Similarly, if an author does not intend effects that are incorporated into his discourse the notion of author's purpose is again useless.

Notes

1. Theodore M. Bernstein, *Watch Your Language* (New York: Pocket Books, 1965), pp. 2–3.

2. From "Speech of Acceptance upon the Award of the Nobel Prize for Literature" by William Faulkner, in *The Faulkner Reader* (New York: Random House, 1954).

3. Discussion of this mode of inquiry appears, among other places, in the writings that follow: Wayne C. Booth, *The Rhetoric of Fiction* (Chicago and London: University of Chicago Press, 1961); R. S. Crane, ed., *Critics and Criticism: Ancient and Modern* (Chicago and London: University of Chicago Press, 1953); R. S. Crane, ed., *Critics and Criticism* (abridged edition; Chicago and London: University of Chicago Press, 1957); R. S. Crane, ed., *The Languages of Criticism and the Structure of Poetry* (Canada: University of Toronto Press, 1957); David H. Richter, *Fable's End: Completeness and Closure in Rhetorical Fiction* (Chicago and London: University of Chicago Press, 1974); Sheldon Sacks, *Fiction and the Shape of Belief* (Berkeley: University of California Press, 1964).

4. Richard McKeon, "Rhetoric and Poetics in the Philosophy of Aristotle," in *Aristotle's Poetics and English Literature,* ed. Elder Olson (Chicago: University of Chicago Press, 1965), p. 231.

5. *The New York Times,* Oct. 20, 1970, p. 42.

6. Joseph F. Hannan, *Never Tease a Dinosaur* (New York: Holt, Rinehart and Winston), p. 30.

CHAPTER 3

EVALUATION AND ITS USES

Chapter 1 introduces the topic of evaluation. Chapter 2 discusses some skills of comprehension. In this chapter the comprehension skills are used to explain and illustrate in some detail the particularities of evaluation. The chapter also discusses the uses that justify the evaluation process and some related issues.

The process and uses of evaluation

The first chapter defines evaluation as a process of determining the extent to which outcomes desired match outcomes achieved.[1] "Desired outcomes" refer to the achievements of students expressed as Level 3 objectives. Among other matters, this chapter explains how to write a test for the skills of comprehension noted in Chapter 2. The explanation is intended to convey not only a clearer understanding of comprehension and its testing, but also a clearer understanding of testing and evaluation generally. The principles explained in this chapter, therefore, may be used to develop instruments and procedures for evaluating programs in the comprehension of literature and to plan and execute any program of evaluation whatsoever.

The procedure for evaluating any program of instruction may be described as a five-step process, as shown in the accompanying table.

THE PROCESS OF EVALUATION

1. Obtain a statement of the Level 3 objectives. If one is not available, formulate it.
2. Select or devise exercises, problems, or other tasks that give the student the opportunity to exhibit the achievements specified by the objectives.
3. Administer the set of evaluative tasks.
4. Obtain a record of the student's performance.
5. Determine from the record the extent to which the performance exhibited matches the performance desired.

An important use of evaluation is the improvement of teaching. Specifically, the results of evaluation may be used to diagnose and improve whatever shortcomings in the program an evaluation reveals. If there is no evaluation, then attempts to improve teaching become matters of subjective impression and the playing of hunches.

Some basic principles

A test that is based upon particular skills or other achievements is called a criterion test because the skills specify the criteria for writing the questions, problems, or other items. Put another way, the skills sought through teaching prescribe the kind of items that must be written. Other terms for such a test are "criterion-referenced" and "criterion-related." In this chapter I explain how to write a criterion test for the comprehension skills described in Chapter 2. This explanation illustrates evaluation in action. But first to some related matters.

During any unit of instruction, evaluation should occur at least three times: at the beginning, to diagnose the students' strengths and weaknesses; toward the middle, to assess progress and to make needed adjustments; at the end, to evaluate the program as a whole and to compile information for improving instruction, informing the administration and community of progress, and, perhaps, informing the profession at large of the contributions to teaching that the program may offer. These procedures and uses of evaluation apply to all instruction.

Because objectives determine evaluation, not all evaluation takes the form of a paper and pencil test. If speech is the goal, then the evaluative situation must put the student to work speaking, and his performance must be judged by appropriate criteria that are sufficiently explicit to guide the assessment. If group discussion is the objective, a similar procedure would be used.

For these two kinds of objectives, the students' performances are recorded by teachers or other evaluators. These may be written comments that specify the extent to which the learner's performance matches the desired performance. In paper and pencil tests, what the students write becomes the records of their performances.

Testing for the literal-sense objective

Evaluation, we have noted, properly begins with a statement of the desired achievements. The literal-sense objective means inferring from a piece of writing what, essentially, it is saying. A related evaluative situation consists of presenting a suitable passage and asking the student to infer just that. Passages may be selected from books, pamphlets, handouts, magazines that the students have, or any other source. Students should be asked to defend their answers by referring to the related particularities of the passage. In the section "Literal-Sense Comprehension," I cite such a passage and sample answers. The teacher's noting the results and discussing these with the class will yield information for revising the program. Revisions may include the selection or more interesting passages at a more fitting level of difficulty, a different emphasis in teaching, and clearer formulations of directions and items in the test.

Testing for the part-whole objective

The part-whole skills discussed in Chapter 2 are the basis for evaluating the teaching of those skills. Essentially, to write a criterion test is to translate the skills into exercises. An exercise has a counterpart in the student's activity when he performs it. One of the skills is inferring the intended effects of an argument. The corresponding test item, therefore, must consist of a passage presenting an argument and directions for the student to identify its intended effects.

The problem of selecting passages leads to our realizing that the part-whole skills and other statements of comprehension skills are actually abstractions. This becomes clear as soon as we realize that the skills refer equally to *The How* and *Why Wonder Book of Dinosaurs* and to *Critique of Judgment* by Immanuel Kant. The materials to be read, therefore, determine the practical consequences of the skills.

To illustrate the process of writing test items, I shall assume that we are concerned with the comprehension of argumentative prose suited to typical students in grade nine. The part-whole skills and the checklist for writing a criterion test clarify just what we are testing for.

The order in the checklist follows that in the table of skills. Notice that each of the parts requires two items. The item labeled A refers to identifying the part; the item labeled B refers to the function of the part, either within the whole or in producing the effects. Items 1 and 2 do not refer directly to the discourse itself, but rather to its intended effects (item 1) and to the audience upon whom the effects are to be produced (item 2). Item 3 refers to the main explanation or argument, and items 4 to 13, to the nonverbal parts. The items that refer to attitude of the author toward himself, his topic, and his audience require a special note: As I mentioned in Chapter 2, attitude toward only one of these three is usually dominant; I suggest that a test refer only to this one dominant attitude.

A test may be written in a number of formats: essay, multiple-choice, true-false, and so on. I suggest that teachers use essay tests, for this reason: the technicalities required to write a test in formats other than the essay make it most unlikely that a busy teacher without technical assistance can write a good machine-scorable test. Although it takes a lot of time to read and evaluate responses to essay questions, it is at least as time-consuming to write a defensible test in a format other than the essay and less likely that the test will be good. To test this assertion, write a short multiple-choice or true-false test on anything; administer it to students and then score the test. Return the test to the students and discuss the results. A free and honest discussion almost certainly will reveal appalling ambiguities in certain items. Although I suggest the use of essay tests, at the same time I acknowledge that complicated skills and abilities are and may be tested by using formats other than the essay. I

CHECKLIST FOR WRITING A CRITERION TEST OF READING COMPREHENSION

1. Purpose or intended effects
2. Audience
3. Main explanation or argument—A
4. Main explanation or argument—B
5. Representation—A
6. Representation—B
7. Attitude—A
8. Attitude—B
9. Details—A
10. Details—B
11. Order—A
12. Order—B
13. Emphasis—A
14. Emphasis—B

justify the suggestion not because the essay format is intrinsically better than others, but rather because it is more likely that teachers will do better with the essay form.

It is both legitimate and advantageous to use the same passage and the same occasion for testing written composition as well as comprehension. (Chapter 5 discusses the teaching and evaluation of composition). If composition and comprehension are to be tested at the same time, allow time enough for the students to compose their answers carefully.

Unless speed of comprehension or of composition is an objective, there is nothing in any reputable theory of evaluation to suggest that testing be harassing. Rather, the respectable theories of curriculum, instruction, and evaluation imply that with objectives clarified and the teaching carefully matched to these and to the interests and capacities of students, the test should come as a welcome opportunity for students to exhibit what they have learned.

It is always a good plan to try out tests and other materials on a sample of the students. The sample may consist of one student who is representative of the members of the class. From this tryout, revise until the bugs are removed.

When the skills to be tested are stated clearly, they may serve as essay questions. Therefore, one plan for writing a criterion test is simply to provide each student with a copy of a passage and a copy of the part-whole skills. Then let the statements of skills put the students to work identifying effects and audience, as well as the parts and their respective functions. Chapter 2 gives examples of desired questions and replies.

Following is an example of a teacher-made criterion test of the kind now being discussed. The questions are based on the part-whole skills. On the assumption that it may be used as a pretest, I have avoided the use of "purpose" because of its ambiguity: The use of "purpose" in this book does not always correspond to general usage. Some people for example, would use "purpose" to mean the main argument. Similarly, I have avoided any term that a student unacquainted with part-whole comprehension is likely to misunderstand. Notice that the "B-type" questions are incorporated into the test, that only the one dominant "attitude" is considered, and that "details" and "order" are treated together. The numbers following each item correspond to the numbers on the checklist for writing a test of this kind.

In preparing a test, the teacher should write the items so that they are comprehensible to his students. He may do this by trying out the test on a student who is typical of those in the class to be tested. The items should be revised until they are satisfactory.

Test on Part-Whole Comprehension

Directions: A selection to be read and a set of questions follow. Read the selection and answer the questions.

Lariats

It frequently happens upon long journeys that the lariat ropes wear out or are lost, and if there were no means of replacing them great inconvenience might result therefrom. A very good substitute may be made by taking the green hide of a buffalo, horse, mule, or ox, stretching it upon the ground, and pinning it down by the edges. After it has been well stretched, a circle is described with a piece of charcoal, embracing as much of the skin as practicable, and a strip about an inch wide cut from the outer edge of sufficient length to form the lariat. The strip is then wrapped around between two trees or stakes, drawn tight, and left to dry, after which it is subjected to a process of friction until it becomes pliable, when it is ready for use; this lariat answers well so long as it is kept dry, but after it has been wet and dried again it becomes very hard and unyielding. This, however, may be obviated by boiling it in oil or grease until thoroughly saturated, after which it remains pliable.

The Indians make very good lariat ropes of dressed buffalo or buck skins cut into narrow strips and braided; these, when oiled, slip much more freely than the hemp or cotton ropes, and are better for lassoing animals, but they are not as suitable for picketing as those made of other material, because the wolves will eat them, and thus set free the animals to which they are attached.[2]

Questions

1. What is the selection intended to do for the reader? (1)
2. What kind of person has this selection been written for? (2)
3. In one sentence, explain what this selection is mainly saying. (3)
4. What this selection is mainly saying helps it produce the effects upon the reader that you describe in Question 1 above. Explain how. (4)
5. What kind of person is the writer? (5)
6. How does the writer's being that kind of person help the selection do the work it is intended to do? This work is to produce the effects you describe in Question 1 above. (6)
7. How does the writer feel toward his reader? (7)
8. How does this feeling or attitude help the selection do its work? (8)
9. What important details are presented and in what order? (9, 11)
10. How do these details and their order in which they appear help the selection do its work? (10, 12)
11. Which detail or set of details is emphasized? (13)
12. How does this emphasis help the selection do its work? (14)

Not only do the part-whole skills specify the items, they also specify the criteria against which the teacher or other evaluator determines the adequacy of the replies. Referring, for example, to checklist items 13 and 14, we would determine the extent to which the student has identified what is most emphasized in the passage and how that emphasis functions. It is legitimate for a student to view a part as functioning in either of two senses: he may show the sense in which the part functions within the argument as a whole, or the sense in which it is a means to effects. Both views of function amount to the same thing. In a passage cited in Chapter 2, the author stressed his annoyance. Within the whole, the emphasis is a means of showing that the traffic between classroom and nurse's office can be trying. As an intended effect upon the reader, that emphasis is a means of persuading the reader of his annoyance. Because both notions of the function of parts share a common element, the student's identifying either shows that he understands.

For further information on the writing and uses of tests and other means of evaluation, I refer the reader to any standard book on testing and evaluation. Most of these, unfortunately, stress standardized tests, a kind that is not intended to assess a particular program by using its Level 3 objectives. To read typical texts on evaluation critically and to think clearly about evaluative issues, one needs to distinguish criterion tests from normed or standardized tests.

Distinguishing criterion from normed tests

Criterion tests, it has been shown, should be part and parcel of classroom instruction. These tests are different from those known by such terms as "normed," "standardized," "norm-related," and "norm-referenced."

Basically, normed tests differ from criterion tests in the sense that each serves a different purpose. As explained, a criterion test is intended to elicit the particular skills or capabilities that students are expected to acquire or possess. But normed tests are designed to reveal, first, the performance of one student in relation to others and, second, the spread of scores within a group of test takers.

A properly constructed normed test, when it is administered, say, to a class of unselected ninth graders, will yield a set of scores whose pattern follows the well-known bell-shaped curve. Only when a test discriminates among students does it work as a norm-related test. Such a test, therefore, is not intended to reveal directly and conveniently just what a student knows and can do. Because a criterion test is designed, purely and simply, to determine what students know or can do, the bell-shaped curve is not a principle by which a criterion test is written.

This distinction between normed and criterion tests is illustrated, rather pointedly, by an evaluation program called "National Assessment of Educational Progress" (NAEP). Its purpose is to provide an index of the nation's educational system, just as the Gross National Product (GNP) is an index of the nation's economic system. Criterion tests are used in the NAEP.

When the idea of a national assessment was first publicized, some educators argued that standardized tests for reading, writing, arithmetic, and so forth indicate what the educational system is doing. But the standardized tests, as noted, are designed to show individual differences. It is criterion tests that show the actual abilities sought by programs of education.[3]

Criterion tests and mastery learning

Tests written from Level 3 objectives are sometimes called mastery tests as well as criterion tests. A criterion test may be so written that it assesses reliably all the achievements sought by a unit of instruction. If a student gets 85 per cent of the items right on such a test, he may be said to have achieved mastery; the other 15 per cent, we may say, allows for the lapses common to all people. A practicable definition of mastery is, of course, only an approximation.

Benjamin S. Bloom and his associates at The University of Chicago have been investigating the possibilities and problems of mastery learning. The assumption of its advocates is that some 90 per cent of students can learn what is taught provided the teacher clarifies his Level 3 objectives, uses appropriate means to attain the learning, evaluates often, and adjusts the instruction from the information that the criterion tests reveal.

Bloom gives good reasons for rejecting the familiar practice of grading on a curve. The bell-shaped curve, he argues, is the model for random activity. Because teaching is a purposeful activity, there is reason to suppose that teaching is unsuccessful if assessments of achievement correspond to the model of randomness. Further inquiry into mastery learning may begin with the Bloom reference appearing in the notes to this chapter.[4]

Evaluation of the student teacher and the in-service teacher

Although this is not a text on supervision, it is instructive to consider the problem of evaluating a teacher. Whether he is a student teacher or an in-service teacher, the principles by which he is properly evaluated are the same. Because the evaluation of teaching is widely misconceived and the misconceptions have serious consequences, the problem is of first importance. Not only may discussion of the problem shed light on evaluating preservice and in-service teachers, it may also clarify the principles of evaluation.

To begin, there is a difference between the evaluation of a teacher and the evaluation of teaching. We have already considered the evaluation of teaching or of programs of instruction. The main purpose for evaluating instruction is to improve it. In evaluating a teacher the purpose includes the improvement of instruction as well as the professional growth of the teacher. With so much at stake, the teacher and the school have much to gain by explicit and proper assessment. Moreover, a fundamental right of a professional or anyone else is sound judgment of his work.

One basis by which teachers are evaluated or misevaluated is opinion, often that of administrative superiors. Sometimes criteria of judgment are formulated as checklists. An examination of a particular checklist will reveal whether its items issue from proper evaluative principles, from a stereotype of what teaching is supposed to look like, or from some other source.

However that may be, when a teacher is judged by opinions of peers or administrative supervisors, the process is sometimes called "professional judgment." There are occasions when such terms as "professional judgment," or "peer judgment" is used to give an aura of respectability to dubious evaluation.

Another procedure, commonly called "evaluation," is that

of students giving their opinions of the teacher and his work. Usually, the process is one in which the students check items on a list that, supposedly, indicates the virtues of a teacher: "Is he well prepared for his classes?" "Does he have a sense of humor?" And so forth. There may be space in such an instrument for the student to add whatever he wishes. Such instruments, also, are means for eliciting opinion. There is, of course, a difference between an *opinion about* teaching and an *evaluation of* teaching.

The following comments about the two procedures described seem appropriate: When opinion is the criterion for evaluating a teacher, it is opinion that will tend to influence the performance. If the eliciting of such opinion should contribute to proper evaluation, then the process is defensible. If, however, such an evaluation is lacking, then the process is invalid.

A third mode of assessment is the use of achievements of students as the criterion. That students learn what they have been taught is the ultimate criterion of a teacher's success. But such achievement does not imply that a teacher is properly evaluated by that criterion. The reason is that an art, and teaching is an art, is evaluated by its principles, not its effects, and it may be unsuccessful even when properly exercised.[5] Aristotle explains further in his description of the rhetorician's task:

> It is clear that [the function of rhetoric] is not simply to succeed in persuading, but rather to discover the means of coming as near such success as the circumstances of each particular case allow. In this it resembles all other arts.
> For example, it is not the function of medicine simply to make a man quite healthy, but to put him as far as may be on the road to health; it is possible to give excellent treatment even to those who can never enjoy sound health.[6]

This argument becomes even more convincing when we consider the history of almost any art. A handy example is the unfavorable reception of Beethoven's Third Symphony when it was first performed, which explains further why an art is properly judged by its principles or methods and not by its effects. And as Aristotle implies, when a patient suffering from an incurable disease dies, that death in itself does not raise questions about his doctor's competence.

In judging a teacher, therefore, the proper criteria are the principles of teaching. In this view he is successful to the extent to which these are incorporated into his practice. Although there is no simple way to evaluate a teacher, there are, as suggested, proper and explicit principles for guiding the task. When both the teacher to be evaluated and those responsible for evaluating understand the criteria, which ought to be clearly stated and understood, there is some chance for the process to become rewarding and humane.

Criterion evaluation and the ultimate aim of schools

Ultimately, the purpose of schools is to help make people and society better. Improved morality, in other words, is the ultimate aim. Morality implies overt behavior, particularly certain kinds of habitual actions: co-operation, helpfulness, efforts to improve conditions at hand, and so forth. Habits, however, cannot be acquired through direct instruction; they are formed only through their exercise.

Education in general and an English class in particular work toward this ultimate aim indirectly: If, for example, competition is eliminated and the classroom conceived as a co-operative community of learners, then conditions are established in which students may be encouraged to help each other rather than compete. Criterion-related evaluation helps provide such conditions. It fosters the meeting of criteria (or the achievement of objectives) rather than the outscoring of others. Working under these conditions, a teacher will offer helpful diagnostic comments on written exercises, tests, and examinations rather than letter grades and numerical scores. My experience shows that in such a class, students will come to reverse their usual expectations by accepting and expecting diagnostic help and resenting grades.

Ideally, when activities are conducted in such a manner, the learning of comprehension, writing, and so on is the aim and improved morality the consequence. It is in this sense that education achieves its ultimate aim indirectly.

Pitfalls

A common distortion of the evaluative process is the writing of examinations without reference to objectives. As an example, consider a teacher who begins with a poem, essay, story, or any other kind of content and simply translates parts of it into questions or other exercises without using Level 3 objectives as criteria for writing the items. If asked to justify such an item, the teacher is likely to say that it is a way of testing for "insight" or "understanding" of whatever the content may be.

The two preceding chapters show that in any rational view of teaching, one tries to clarify just what he means by "insight" or "understanding," and expresses these as Level 3 objectives, which serve him as guides. Often it happens that a teacher clarifies his purposes in the midst of teaching or as a consequence of it. The subsequent teaching, then, would be guided by this further clarification. But a final evaluation is hardly the occasion to test for what has not yet been systematically taught.

Like the first, the second degradation is also a kind of mismatch between objective and item of evaluation. In this second kind of malpractice, the teacher might begin with the objective, "Identify techniques of persuasion in printed advertisements," and write as an evaluation item "Write an advertisement using five techniques of persuasion." Writing an ad goes beyond identifying techniques of persuasion. If the writing of ads is the desired outcome, then this ability should be formulated as an objective, a program devised for the teaching of it, and the program evaluated. Students and everyone else concerned with evaluation have every right to expect a correspondence among objectives, instruction, and evaluation.

A third perversion is the practice of evaluating instruction by means of normed tests. Again, this is a mismatch between evaluation and objectives.

Summary

1. Evaluation is a process of assessing the extent to which outcomes achieved match outcomes desired.

2. A five-step procedure explains the process of evaluation.

3. The main purpose of evaluation is the improvement of teaching. Other purposes include those of informing the community, the school as a whole, and the profession of the results of teaching.

4. The distinction between criterion and normed tests clarifies some misleading and wrong notions about the results of teaching.

5. Criterion testing is indispensable to carefully-monitored teaching, which includes "mastery learning."

6. Probably most criteria for evaluating student teachers and in-service teachers are dubious. The proper criteria for such evaluation, however, have been available at least since classical antiquity.

7. Criterion testing or evaluation is one means by which the school may achieve its ultimate purpose, which is a moral one and is indirectly attained.

Exercises

Exercise 1

Write an essay-type criterion test for the fourteen skills of part-whole comprehension. Use four passages and divide the number of questions in some such pattern as these: 3 4 3 4, 4 4 4 2. The level of difficulty of the passages should be at a year of schooling in which you are interested. To get an idea of difficulty level, examine the nonfiction prose in anthologies used at this school level.

Exercise 2

Should students in junior and senior high schools be graded on a curve? Why or why not? If not, what criteria for grading them should be used? Identify your position on this issue clearly and justify your stand.

Exercise 3

Does Chapter 3 imply that grading is evaluation? Can there be evaluation without grading of students? Explain.

Exercise 4

Directions: Comment on the following in terms of the principles discussed in this and earlier chapters. Be sure to comment on the items italicized and on any other aspect of this discourse. Your discussion should provide evidence that you understand the principles underlying the issues. Therefore, justify your comments by reference to the principles related to the issue. Do not conceive this to be an empty "my opinion vs. your opinion" discussion. Rather conceive it as an opportunity for you to show that you can identify issues, relate these to the principles underlying them, and argue not from hunches but from principles.

Greetings to the new ninth-grade teachers of Jupiter Junior High School. The Jupiter School District is committed to the new and the innovative. For example, every teacher who we hire is committed to an open (1) *system of student evaluation of teaching*. After all, your students are with you most of the day and therefore they know best how good or how bad your teaching is.

During the first part of the year (2) *your objective is to teach literature*. You will be given sets of anthologies to use as well as a state syllabus. The following poems and stories must be taught in the order listed: [The list follows, but is omitted here.] This list has been developed by people higher in the hierarchy than you. Therefore, (3) *to deviate from this list would be a failure of professional discipline because, clearly, the job of the teacher is to do what the curriculum guides say he must do.*

The best way to achieve the objective is to (4) *cover the material*. You will find the questions at the ends of the selections useful in covering the material.

Of course, the best way to evaluate would be to (5) *take the material that you cover and translate some of that material into multiple-choice questions or essay questions.* Be sure that some of the questions are hard and some easy. (6) *After all what other basis is there for making a test?*

Certainly (7) *the only reason for giving a test is to decide how to grade the students.* We are an advanced district; we therefore use computers. Here's how things work. (8) *We give grades each month as well as midterm and final examinations. We feed these scores into the computer. We give some added weight to the midterm and final and then the computer figures out the average for each student, which becomes his final grade.* (9) *Evaluation, of course, means finding out who is doing well, who is doing badly, and who is doing middling work,* and we feel that we have arrived at a fair and equitable system of evaluation.

Exercise 5

Here are some Level 3 objectives. Describe an evaluative situation appropriate to each.

Identify the main argument in newspaper editorials.

Explain devices of persuasion in advertisements.

Deliver persuasive speeches.

Notes

1. This chapter extends the discussion begun in Chapter 1. The conception of evaluation, then, is that presented in Tyler's *Basic Principles of Curriculum and Instruction* (Chicago: University of Chicago Press, 1950), pp. 68–81.

2. Randolph B. Marcy, *The Prairie Traveler: A Handbook for Overland Expeditions* (New York: Harper & Bros., 1859), pp. 161–62.

3. For further discussion of this issue, see Ralph W. Tyler, "The Federal Role in Education," *The Public Interest,* 34 (Autumn 1975), 164–87.

4. Benjamin S. Bloom, J. Thomas Hastings, and George S. Madaus, "Learning for Mastery," in *Handbook on Formative and Summative Evaluation of Student Learning* (New York: McGraw-Hill, 1971), pp. 43–57.

5. Richard McKeon, "Rhetoric and Poetics in the Philosophy of Aristotle," in *Aristotle's Poetics and English Literature,* ed. Elder Olson (Chicago: University of Chicago Press, 1965), p. 231.

6. Aristotle *Rhetoric* 1.1355[b] i.10

CHAPTER 4

THE ANALYSIS OF IDEAS

Arguments, in this chapter, are taken to be examples of reasoning. The assumption is explained and procedures for teaching are illustrated.

Three modes of comprehension

Chapter 2 cites three properties of arguments with which this book is concerned. The rest of that chapter examines two in some detail. This chapter discusses the third. To set the stage, I remind the reader of all three properties. First, an argument says something literally, which implies literal-sense comprehension. Second, an argument communicates, which implies part-whole comprehension. Third, an argument exhibits a process of reasoning, which implies the analysis of ideas.

Explaining further, I shall illustrate briefly and oversimply the first two of these methods and explain the third more fully. The document popularly called the Declaration of Independence will serve as an illustrative text.

In its literal sense the Declaration says that for certain reasons the Thirteen United Colonies have dissolved "the political bands which have connected them with . . . the state of Great Britain" and have become a separate, independent nation. Considered as persuasion, the document is intended to produce such effects upon "the opinions of mankind" that the world may be persuaded of "the rectitude of our intentions."

Literal-sense comprehension, then, is aimed at identifying the main argument, while part-whole comprehension includes that aim as well as those of identifying and explaining the causes or parts incorporated into discourses by which persuasion is effected. As mentioned, Chapter 2 treats such matters in some detail.

The logical basis of the analysis of ideas[1]

Following Elder Olson, this chapter conceives the analysis of ideas as a procedure governed by five postulates.

1. The starting point is this assumption: any argument, viewed purely as reasoning, is intended to resolve an issue or answer a question. The purpose of an argument, therefore, is to resolve the question that it intends to answer. Notice that in analysis of ideas, we do not assume, as we do in part-whole comprehension, that producing effects upon the reader is the purpose. Our assumption does not deny, however, that a cogent argument is a main cause of persuasion. And no inconsistency is involved when we examine the reasoning in an argument without reference to its persuasive powers. I suggest this separation of persuasion from reason as a pedagogical device for the specific teaching of the analysis of ideas, but this does not imply that such separation characterizes the practice of good readers. Because the purpose is to resolve a question, the argument itself ends when the question is really or apparently resolved.

2. The assumption that the purpose is to answer a question implies, further, that the question be inferred and explained from the argument, which must be the primary source for clarifying the question. At all times, then, the argument is considered a means by which the question is resolved.

3. An extended inquiry requires a set of subproblems. The argument, therefore, must be divided according to these in its main divisions and divided into further subdivisions if these main divisions have subsidiaries.

4. Every device—distinction, definition, example, quotation, and so on—is used deliberately. Each use of these is to be explained in terms of its function in resolving the question and as a sign of what the author considers to be his demonstration or his method of inquiry.

5. As with devices, the order of the argument as a whole is to be explained in terms of what the author considers his demonstration or method of inquiry.

Notes on feasibility

In general, the skills implied are those that typical secondary-school students possess and use. Any schoolboy knows that "a mouth full of bloody Chiclets" means "teeth that are knocked out" and he knows the function of that metaphor in whatever context it appears. Basically, teaching the analysis of ideas implies directing the student's attention and his skills of inference to the particular problems that a text presents.

Some of these problems, usually a few, require verification other than inference from context; and other than uses of everyday knowledge, as our Chiclets metaphor suggests. For example, meaning of "all men are created equal" in the Declaration of Independence cannot be inferred from the context. Taken quite literally, the statement cannot be true because no one denies that people vary widely in physical and mental endowment and in social and economic advantage.

Further inquiry, therefore, is required. When a problem arises, we go to the specialist. Historians know that the writer of the Declaration, Thomas Jefferson, took his idea of equality from John Locke's *Second Treatise on Government,* which explains Jefferson's use of the term and the meaning of the clause: all, equally, are entitled to protection of their lives, their liberty, and their pursuit of happiness.

A formulation of the ideas and skills

The accompanying table presents a formulation of the analysis of ideas as sets of assumptions, corollaries, and skills.

ANALYSIS OF IDEAS: THE OPERATIONAL PRINCIPLES

1. *Assumptions and corollaries*
   1.1. Assumptions
      1.11. An argument is an answer to a question.
      1.12. Words and statements are vague and equivocal prior to, and separate from, verification and interpretation.
   1.2. Corollaries
      1.21. Within an argument, the senses in which words and terms are used may be only remotely related to common usage and definition in dictionaries.
      1.22. Within an argument, the meanings of terms and statements are determined by their relationship to other terms and statements, as is the question that the argument answers.
2. *Skills*
   2.1. Identify the precise question to which the argument is an answer.
   2.2. Identify the answer.
   2.3. Explain the method of reasoning by which the argument moves from the question to the answer. In the explanation, account for the following:
      2.31. The senses in which the author uses his terms and distinctions.
      2.32. The unstated assumptions.
      2.33. The sections into which the argument is divided.
      2.34. The sequence in which these sections appear.
      2.35. The examples, citations, distinctions, and so on.
      2.36. The functions of 2.31–2.35 within the argument.

It has been deduced from the five postulates and it is intended to guide teaching.

Beginning the inquiry

Teaching to infer the question that an argument answers is one way to begin. Select lots of slogans, aphorisms, and other short arguments. Present these to the class orally or in writing. For each one, ask, "What is the question to which this argument is intended to be a reply?"

The same acceptable answer will be expressed differently by different students. Here are some examples of arguments (answers to the first two are supplied):

Honesty is the best policy. (What is the best policy? or What is the best policy for guiding our actions?)

A stitch in time saves nine. (When should repairs be made?)

To wrong those we hate is to add fuel to our hatred. Conversely, to treat an enemy with magnanimity is to blunt our hatred for him.[2]

A man is likely to mind his own business when it is worth minding. When it is not, he takes his mind off his own meaningless affairs by minding other people's business.

This minding of other people's business expresses itself in gossip, snooping, and meddling, and also in feverish interest in communal, national, and racial affairs. In running away from ourselves we either fall on our neighbor's shoulder or fly at his throat.[3]

In the discussion, maintain a distinction between the question that the argument answers and matters of agreement, disagreement, and importance with respect to the ideas and issues that the argument raises. The selections may be gradually increased in length and complexity. Newspapers, everyday conversation, aphorisms, and slogans are some of the sources from which a limitless selection may be made. There is no need or reason to depend on typical schoolroom materials. Adapt teaching to the concerns of the moment.

The ability to infer what an author means by his terms and distinctions may be developed through appropriate materials, questions, and discussion. Select materials in which (1) the readability and ideas are suited to the group and (2) some terms are used in senses that are out of the ordinary. Then conduct a discussion through which the students infer the meanings of the out-of-the-ordinary terms.

In the selection that follows, for example, V. I. Lenin describes, metaphorically, one of the early struggles of the Russian revolutionists. On the assumption that the class has access to the selection, ask them to read it and to be prepared to explain the meanings *within the text* of "a compact group," "holding each other by the hand," "enemies," "their almost constant fire," "marsh," and "free."

We are marching in a compact group along a precipitous and difficult path, firmly holding each other by the hand. We are surrounded on all sides by enemies, and we have to advance under their almost constant fire. We have combined voluntarily, precisely for the purpose of fighting the enemy, and not to retreat into the adjacent marsh, the inhabitants of which, from the very outset, have reproached us with having separated ourselves into an exclusive group and with having chosen the path of struggle instead of the path of conciliation. And now several among us begin to cry out: let us go into this marsh! And when we begin to shame them, they retort: how conservative you are! Are you not ashamed to deny us the liberty to invite you to take a better road! Oh, yes, gentlemen! You are free not only to invite us, but to go yourselves wherever you will, even into the marsh. In fact, we think that the marsh is your proper place, and we are prepared to render *you* every assistance to get there. Only let go of our hands, don't clutch at us and don't besmirch the grand word "freedom," for we too are "free" to go where we please, free to fight not only against the marsh, but also against those who are turning toward the marsh![4]

As a result of the discussion, one of the conclusions that the class should reach is that the term, "free," in Lenin's text has a meaning quite opposite to that of individual liberty. The discussion, further, should clarify the function of the metaphor of the marching group amidst the enemy: it functions as a device to explain why in this view the group, but not the individual, is "free."

In teaching to identify unstated assumptions, ask the class to explain what it is that joins two such sentences as the following into a single, unified argument:

Large numbers of our students smoke pot. Therefore, our students should be required to take a course in drug abuse.

The discussion should lead to the inference that the assumption is "The taking of a course in drug abuse will (or is likely to) decrease the practice of misusing drugs." Whether the assumption is acceptable would be a topic for further discussion. The class may need to be reminded that an argument may be coherent but not defensible.

A restatement of the skill that we are now considering is "Explain the logical steps by which an argument moves." The unstated steps in the logical progression must be explained as unstated assumptions. Consider, for example, the following argument:

Our students are ripping off local merchants. Therefore, we should teach courses in morality.

In the following restatement, two of the unstated assumptions are inserted as the second and third sentences:

Our students are ripping off local merchants. A duty of schools is to help make people moral. Morality can be directly taught and learned. Therefore, we should teach courses in morality.

With assumptions clarified, there is an increase in the accessibility of the argument to reasoned discussion and critical response. The reason is that the intelligibility of an argument not only depends on the clarity of its overt statements but on the explicitness of its unstated assumptions as well. It may help to say that these assumptions may be viewed as the glue that binds an argument together.

The three arguments listed below suggest the range of materials suited to the inferring of unstated assumptions and the ease with which the materials may be selected and devised:

> Many truck drivers eat at the Blue Angel Diner. That means that the food there must be good.

> People are losing interest in religion. Proof of this is to be found in the declining attendance in churches and synagogues.

> Because people spend fewer hours reading and writing than they do watching television, learning to read and write is less important than it used to be.

Applying the skills to a particular selection

This chapter continues by explaining, through illustration, the use of all the skills. The text is a carefully written letter of dubious morality but of some importance in recent history. First, then, the letter; next, questions implied by the skills to be taught along with desired answers.

Nixon Letter to Ervin

Dear Mr. Chairman:

I have considered your request that I permit the committee to have access to tapes of my private conversations with a number of my closest aides. I have concluded that the principles stated in my letter to you of July 6th preclude me from complying with that request, and I shall not do so. Indeed the special nature of tape recordings of private conversations is such that these principles apply with even greater force to tapes of private Presidential conversations than to Presidential papers.

If release of the tapes would settle the central questions at issue in the Watergate inquiries, then their disclosure might serve a substantial public interest that would have to be weighed very heavily against the negatives of disclosure.

The fact is that the tapes would not finally settle the central issues before your committee. Before their existence became publicly known, I personally listened to a number of them. The tapes are entirely consistent with what I know to be the truth and what I have stated to be the truth. However, as in any verbatim recording of informal conversations, they contain comments that persons with different perspectives and motivations would inevitably interpret in different ways. Furthermore, there are inseparably interspersed in them a great many very frank and very private comments, on a wide range of issues and individuals, wholly extraneous to the committee's inquiry.

Even more important, the tapes could be accurately understood or interpreted only by reference to an enormous number of other documents and tapes, so that to open them all would begin an endless process of disclosure and explanation of private Presidential records totally unrelated to Watergate, and highly confidential in nature. They are the clearest possible example of why Presidential documents must be kept confidential.

Accordingly, the tapes, which have been under my sole control, will remain so. None has been transcribed or made public and none will be.

On May 22d I described my knowledge of the Watergate matter and its aftermath in categorical and unambiguous terms that I know to be true. In my letter of July 6th, I informed you that at an appropriate time during the hearings I intend to address publicly the subjects you are considering. I still intend to do so and in a way that preserves the constitutional principle of separation of powers, and thus serves the interest not just of Congress or of the President, but of the people.

> Sincerely,
> Richard Nixon (signed)[5]

The questions that follow correspond to the skills that appear in this chapter's table that presents the operational principles.

What is the question that the letter is intended to answer?
(Will the President release the tapes?)

What is the answer? (No.)

The rest of the inquiry is intended to clarify this question:
Through what method of reasoning does the argument
move from the question to the answer? (Basically, there are
four reasons given for refusing to release the tapes. The
reasons and the sequence in which they appear are these:
To release the tapes would

1. Violate the idea of separation of powers
2. Violate the principle of confidentiality
3. Fail to settle the issue
4. Require the prying into other confidential tapes and
   papers, thus making the inquiry useless and
   impractical.)

In the argument are there terms and distinctions used in
out-of-the ordinary senses? (There are two of particular
importance: "separation of powers" and "President."
Typically, "separation of powers" refers to the functions
and powers of the executive, judicial, and legislative
branches of government. The three branches have separate
but related functions so that they will check and balance
one another, thus preventing arbitrary and uncontrolled
use of power. In the letter, however, "check and balance"
is disregarded and "separation of powers" is used to give
an aura of respectability to the President's assumption that
his prerogatives include the withholding of the tapes.
Similarly the term, "President," implies that no verification
of Presidential statements need be permitted.)

What unstated assumptions, if any, are implied? (The
answer just given shows two related assumptions: One is
that the President is free from accountability and the other
is that freedom from accountability is a characteristic of the
Presidency. These assumptions, however, violate the principle of checks and balances.)

Explain the uses of citations or examples. (An example of
some interest is the President's listening to some of the
tapes. It suggests that he considers his own unverified
testimony to serve as proof.)

What function does the sequence of reasons serve? (The first two reasons are theoretical: they refer to violations of a constitutional principle and of confidentiality. The second two are practical: they refer to the release of the tapes' doing no good and the entire notion of their release being impractical. In effect, this sequence of reasons says that release of the tapes is wrong in theory and unfeasible in practice.)

In analyzing the ideas of this argument, the following conclusions are defensible: the argument is based on unacceptable assumptions and unacceptable conceptions of the Presidency and separation of powers; moreover, it disregards checks and balances, a principle without which separation of powers loses its point. As a whole, then, the argument cannot withstand critical examination.

Some applications

The set of skills just explained and illustrated are required for inquiring into discourses of some complexity and importance. Simple-minded diatribes, sentimental reminiscences, or hastily written memoranda hardly require the use of these skills.

In everyday life we meet dubious statements with regrettable frequency. These discourses often offend our sense of justice and affect aspects of our lives. We and our students must be constantly critical and constantly on guard lest our lives be manipulated by the operators. Our instrument of criticism is basically the analysis of ideas.

Suppose, for example, that we find something like this in a school bulletin:

To the Teachers of Jupiter Junior High

The time has come to evaluate teaching. Your students are with you most of the time. Therefore, they are best equipped to evaluate your teaching. Your students will be asked to fill out teacher evaluation forms. And because word of your teaching gets around to your colleagues, they too will be asked to evaluate your teaching.

The entire apparatus of the analysis of ideas is hardly needed to respond critically to such a policy. A determination from context of just what is intended by "evaluate teaching," and "teacher-evaluation form" leads to a dismaying conclusion: the evaluation of teaching in this context means the same thing as opinions about teaching and the method of evaluation means the collecting of opinions. When all this is compared to the evaluative principles described in Chapter 3, we are led to the conclusion that there is a wide discrepancy between sound evaluative theory and the assumptions about evaluation that underlie the statement in our imaginary bulletin.

Again, suppose that we find a regulation in a school that members of athletic teams need not participate in physical education classes required of all able-bodied students. Upon what assumption or assumptions is this regulation grounded? That the physical education classes are not beneficial physically? That such classes offer no physical benefits to team members? That the classes are unpleasant and release from them is a reward granted to team members? Which of these assumptions, if any, or what other assumptions lie behind the regulation?

A democracy requires critical citizens. If powers of criticism are to grow, they must be exercised, not only on advertising and editorials, but also on the school regulation and the grammar text. In Chapter 9 I discuss criticism of grammars. Eternal vigilance, we have been advised, is the price of liberty. And uncriticized enterprises always deteriorate.

But it is not enough merely to understand statements, the assumptions behind them, and to arrive at a critical position. Knowledge and the conviction it develops are sterile unless these become a basis for action. Responsible action requires the following of due process. In a school, due process implies finding the established lines of communication and, within these, attempting to persuade through reason. Other issues of interest to teachers of English and their students appear in the exercises at the end of this chapter.

For teachers and other educators, the analysis of ideas, ideally, has an important place in curricular innovation. If, for example, a subject new to the curriculum is to be taught, then the ideas of that subject need to be analyzed. In particular, its methods, terms, and distinctions must be clarified so that their suitability for teaching may be judged and their use in the curriculum properly treated. An illustration and description of procedure appear in Chapter 9.

Not only is the analysis of ideas a method of comprehension, it is a method of inquiry into ideas and issues generally. These include social, political, and moral problems. Apart from the school-life examples just presented, the letter reprinted in Chapter 2 illustrates the analysis of ideas used to investigate rather than to comprehend. The writer of that letter identifies particular assumptions and ideas relating to crime in New York City and, thereby, suggests a clarification of an aspect of the problem.

Finally, all subjects are presented as arguments. The analysis of ideas is a method for comprehending the particularities of their logic. It follows that this is ultimately a method of independent study and of inquiry into all subjects and issues.

Pitfalls

A widely practiced debasement is the use of an argument not for inferring its author's intention, but for providing a stimulus for its reader's free association. As a result, the misreader becomes misinformed and confused because he imposes on a term or an entire argument what most conveniently comes to mind, or what may help him with a neurosis, or what may help him avoid the hard work of getting at just what its author means.

Thus, the Soviet Union to him may be a democracy in a familiar Western sense because their leaders use "democracy" to describe their form of government. And Chomsky's grammar and Jespersen's grammar "conflict" in his view, although each of these grammarians begin with different assumptions, use different terms and methods of reasoning, and arrive, therefore, at different conclusions. Indeed, the several "conflicts in criticism," "conflicts in curricular inquiry," "conflicts in politics," and so on that he sees may not really be conflicts

A FOUR-CAUSE COMPARISON OF PART-WHOLE ANALYSIS AND ANALYSIS OF IDEAS VIEWED AS METHODS FOR COMPREHENDING ARGUMENTS

Part-whole analysis	Analysis of ideas
The final cause implies that the reader infer the intended effects of the argument.	The final cause implies that the reader infer the question to which an argument is an answer, the answer, and the method of reasoning through which the answer has been derived.
The formal cause implies that the reader infer the argument itself.	The formal cause implies that the reader infer the argument itself.
The efficient cause implies that the reader infer the nonverbal parts and their functions that constitute the argument.	The efficient cause implies that the reader identify the terms and distinctions and the method of reasoning with these through which the argument moves from the question to the answer.
The material cause implies that the reader identify the verbal part or the language in which the nonverbal parts are embodied.	The material cause implies that the reader identify the language in which the argument is embodied.

at all but simply different aspects of an issue treated in different ways.

Not only are such misconceptions caused by failure to identify the intentions of terms, they are caused also by failure to infer unstated assumptions, to identify the question to which the argument speaks, and to realize that ideas take on meaning in the context of a process of reasoning, as Nixon's use of "separation of powers" shows.

Summary

1. As a method for comprehending argument, the analysis of ideas is based on the assumption that an argument demonstrates a process of reasoning. The analytical skills implied require the reader to identify the question or problem that the argument addresses, the answer to that question, the terms in which the problem and the argument is conceived, and the method of reasoning by which the argument moves from the question to the answer.

2. The accompanying table compares the analysis of ideas with part-whole analysis, both viewed as methods for comprehending argument.

3. All school subjects and all proposals, analyses, and discussions on all topics are formulated as arguments. The assumptions and logic of any argument may be clarified through the analysis of ideas. This method, therefore, is appropriate for investigating all subjects and problems, for independent study, and for reading in the content fields.

4. In principle, part-whole analysis has been derived from the analysis of ideas, as have other investigative methods: If, for example, a piece of writing is assumed to be a thing made for a purpose, then an analysis of that assumption together with an analysis of the principles by which discourse is constructed make explicit the parts and skills that constitute part-whole analysis.

5. The distinction between comprehension and inference drawn in Chapter 2 applies also to the analysis of ideas and explains many of its practical uses.

Exercises

Exercise 1

Identify a broad social or ethical problem with which you think secondary-school students are concerned, and then identify appropriate materials through which students may explore this problem. Analyze the ideas of one of the selections. Identify pedagogical problems that are likely to arise and explain how you would deal with these.

Some examples of problems and materials follow:

Problem	*Materials*
Ethics, Law and Order	Charles Frankel, "Is It Ever Right to Break the Law?"[6] Martin Luther King, "Letter from Birmingham Jail."[7]
Patriotism	Abraham Lincoln, "Gettysburg Address." Thomas Paine, "The Crisis" from *Common Sense*.
Individualism	Henry David Thoreau, *Walden*.

Exercise 2

Identify a local school or city policy, law, or regulation that arouses controversy. Explain how you would lead a class to examine the assumptions that underlie the matter and to help each student arrive at a reasoned position on the issue.

Exercise 3

The principle of analysis of ideas may be applied to the resolution of personal problems. In public schools, however, problems of sex and religion are usually *verboten*. By talking to secondary-school students or their teachers identify a problem that concern students. Identify related materials, and propose plans through which students may seek solutions to the problem.

Exercise 4

Assume that you have been teaching the analysis of ideas by means of readings and discussions on the civil disobedience issue and that within the class opinion is sharply divided. How would you evaluate the unit of instruction? To answer this question rationally you must control the principles of evaluation that are stated in Chapter 3 and be clear that the primary aim is the student's increased ability to use these analytical skills.

Exercise 5

Here are a number of terms which in various contexts are presented to teachers of English. From the contexts in which they appear determine what references, if any, they have, whether there is any consistency in their varying uses, and what, if anything, they may contribute to improving the teaching of English.

1. visual literacy.
2. relevance.
3. humanistic (humanistic curriculum, humanistic objective).
4. open education.
5. theme (in literary contexts).
6. tone (in literary contexts).
7. the human condition.
8. any terms that appear in the writings of Marshall McLuhan, e.g., "hot medium," "cool medium," and so forth.
9. formative evaluation.
10. summative evaluation.

Notes

1. This view of the analysis of ideas is taken from Elder Olson, "The Argument of Longinus' *On the Sublime*," in *Critics and Criticism: Ancient and Modern*, ed. R. S. Crane (Chicago and London: University of Chicago Press, 1952), pp. 232ff. The article was first published in *Modern Philology* (February 1942). This method is also described in R. S. Crane, *The Languages of Criticism*

and the *Structure of Poetry* (Toronto: University of Toronto Press, 1953), pp. 10ff.

2. Eric Hoffer, *The True Believer: Thoughts on the Nature of Mass Movements* (Mentor Books; New York: New American Library, 1958), p. 89; first published by Harper and Brothers, 1951.

3. *Ibid.,* p. 23.

4. V. I. Lenin, *What Is to Be Done? Burning Questions of Our Movement* (Moscow: Foreign Languages Publishing House, n.d.), pp. 15–16.

5. Reprinted from *The New York Times,* city edition, July 24, 1973, p. 24.

6. Among other places, the selection appears in *Modern American Essays,* ed. Sylvia Z. Brodkin and Elizabeth J. Pearson (New York: Globe, 1967).

7. *Ibid.*

CHAPTER 5

THE WRITING OF EXPOSITION AND ARGUMENT[1]

On the assumption that written composition is an example of communication, this chapter identifies the skills, presents a catalogue of suggested learning activities, and proposes criteria and procedures by which teachers and students may evaluate compositions.

The objective

A valued result of the study of English is students able to communicate through writing. On the assumption that expository prose is the most widely used form of writing, that form is justifiably the main concern of composition in the English curriculum. This chapter explains and identifies a coherent and comprehensive set of skills that defines the writer's task, suggests activities by which these skills may be improved, and discusses some related pedagogical matters.

The complexity of teaching composition makes it imperative to be clear about what the objective is and is not. For reasons to be explained, I state the overall objective as: "Write expository prose that is likely to produce desired effects upon intended readers." For "expository prose" such words as these may be substituted: "ten-sentence paragraphs," "300-word themes," "essays," "factual articles," "anecdotes." Any of the objectives just stated may be regarded as Level 3.

Some statements on the teaching of composition assert that

the aim is "ordering experience," "organizing thought," or something other than the objective just stated. Such statements imply that composition is a means to some other end. This chapter assumes, however, that programs in written composition are intended to teach writing.

It is important to distinguish principles for constructing discourse, on the one hand, from that which discourse conveys, on the other. The principles of construction are everywhere the same and are understood, consciously or not, by competent writers. This chapter explicates the principles.

Because the principles are available to all, these may be used to convey insight or distortion, wisdom or stupidity. The concern in this chapter is with principles of construction. Skill in the use of these gives the student an instrument of influence and explains the power of the pen. Ultimately, one's education as a whole determines what he writes and for what ends. Although the distinction of principles of construction from what is to be conveyed clarifies the task of teaching composition, the two must finally be brought together. Because improved morality is the ultimate aim of all education, the work in composition must be directed toward that aim. Some specific suggestions appear in the section "Criterion evaluation and the ultimate aim of schools" in Chapter 3 and later in this chapter where evaluation by students is discussed.

In teaching to write, a convenient starting point is the assumption or truism that anyone writes well to the extent that his use of the skills of writing is appropriate to the purpose of his composition. Each of these skills is a constituent of the single overall objective for written composition. A complete inventory of these specifies what is to be taught and learned. The discussion that follows describes that inventory:

Chapter 2 explains the parts of exposition and argument and shows their use in teaching to comprehend. This chapter shows their use in teaching to write. The analysis of ideas may be viewed as probing inquiry into the nonverbal parts of details, order, and emphasis.

To write is to construct all the nonverbal and verbal parts,

THE PRINCIPLES OF WRITING EXPOSITION AND ARGUMENT

1. *Purpose.*
   1.1. Identify a purpose or intended effects for the composition.
   1.2. Identify the perceived reader(s) and make assumptions about him that affect what is written.
2. *Product.*
   2.1. *Form or the whole:* Identify what is to be argued or explained.
   2.2. *Nonverbal parts* (the nonverbal constituents of the whole):
      2.21. Convey a representation of the personal characteristics of the author.
      2.22. Convey an attitude toward the topic, the reader, and himself.
      2.23. Present details such as thoughts, facts, ideas, examples, and so on that are suited to purpose and reader.
      2.24. Organize the details into a sequence.
      2.25. Assign to the details and sections degrees of emphasis. (Equality of emphasis may be justified.)
   2.3. *Verbal part or language* (the verbal constituents of the whole):
      2.31. Select from the resources of the language particular words, sentences, and varieties of usage.
      2.32. Write in a style that is appropriate to writing and to the literary convention, such as essay or article, which is being written.
      2.33. Follow the conventions of the writing system.

each in its own way functioning to affect readers. That does not imply that we tell the student of composition to construct a set of parts. Because any piece of verbal communication necessarily consists of this set, we complicate things by asking that the parts be constructed.

Further, a piece of writing implies skills in the use of two conventions. One refers to spelling, capitalization, punctuation, and the rest; the other convention refers to writing in a style expected not of speech, but of writing.

The skills of writing, then, may be grouped into those of purpose and product. Skills of purpose refer to intended effects and intended reader. Skills of product refer to the main explanation or argument and to the parts of which it is constituted. As explained in Chapter 1, the parts are usefully subdivided into two kinds: nonverbal and verbal.

The foregoing discussion implies the principles of writing, which are presented in the accompanying table.

Some consequences for teaching

Having explained and presented the principles of writing, I find it convenient now to spell out some consequences for teaching.

First, it is a good plan to begin specific and systematic instruction in written composition after the study of part-whole comprehension. The analysis of ideas may be desirable but less imperative. From his study of part-whole comprehension, the student, ideally, is led to the conception of a piece of writing as a made thing, purpose as effects upon readers, and parts as causes of effects. Such a set of ideas, terms, and distinctions provides a basis for coherent inquiry into problems of composition.

Second, this view of a piece of writing suggests a need to reconsider traditional notions about narrowing or limiting a topic. Just about everyone who has studied composition has been taught such ideas as these: "The United States" is a large topic; "Illinois" is also a large topic but smaller than "The United States." Both topics, we have been taught, are too large for a 300-word composition. Therefore, we have been told, it is necessary to "limit" or to "narrow" such topics so that these may be suited to next Tuesday's 300-word assignment. Thus, so the tradition has it, topics that are properly "narrowed" or "limited" may be "My Neighborhood in Chicago" or "The Boys on My Block."

These traditional notions and practices, however, are dubious. Any subject or topic for writing whatsoever permits varying amounts of discourse ranging from limitless to brief. The topic, "Man and His Universe," may be briefly treated if the purpose is to inform the reader of a few facts. Some books for children give brief treatment to big topics. The writer, we have seen, does not really "narrow" or "expand" a topic. Rather, he adapts his means to his purposes and to such exigencies as the space available to him and to other conditions under which he must write.

Third, when a student is writing, he is, consciously or not, practicing the skills of the professional writer, which I assume are those on the foregoing list. Similarly, when he swims the length of the pool, he is doing the things that a champion swimmer does. The difference between the ordinary swimmer and the champion is not essentially in kind but in degree. The same skills of writing are used by both learner and professional in their writing on any and all topics. Therefore, teaching and curriculum plans that are based on the assumption that certain skills of writing should be taught at certain levels of schooling rest on dubious logical and empirical grounds.

Some writers of curriculum plans assume that certain forms and lengths of writing are suited to this school level or that. These assumptions, also, are dubious because the skills of writing are the same regardless of topic, length, grade level, or whatever.

A student's growth in writing, therefore, is his growth toward one or some combination of the skills that to some extent he already possesses. To test this contention, try to determine which skill of purpose or product is omitted when anyone writes and what skill, if any, needs to be added.

Fourth, the facts of human variability imply, and everyday work in the classroom proves, that different students have varying needs. If the items on the list are right, the needs will necessarily refer to one or some combination of those items. No textbook or curriculum guide can predict which needs given students will have at a particular time. The needs of students, not the prescriptions of texts and curriculum guides, properly determine which skills to teach.

Students reveal their needs through what they write. What they were taught or not taught earlier does not determine what their needs are. They may have "finished" a unit on punctuation two years ago, one year ago, or last week. But if their writing today is badly punctuated, a need for teaching is clear. The comma splice and parallel construction may be allotted to next year's composition text or last year's course of study. But it is today that Sally writes: "We were ready at eight o'clock, two hours later the bus picked us up." and "They would rather walk than to drive." The writing of students, not the books or the guides, indicate what they need to learn.

Fifth, clarity of purpose helps a teacher devise flexible arrangements by which to do his work. Although different students have particular needs, classroom instruction is usually a group enterprise. Actually, instructing a class is only one form of teaching. Comment on papers is a second form. The individual or group conference is a third, and peer-group instruction is a fourth. There are no widely accepted criteria for deciding when to use this form or that. The decisions depend on conditions of schools and the preferences and abilities of teachers. There are, however, a few useful practices:

1. An inspection of any set of student papers almost always reveals misunderstandings and other mistakes that are shared by a large percentage of the class. The class as a whole may receive the necessary teaching, which is likely to meet more needs than those revealed by the one set of papers.

2. Members of the class can read and criticize each other's papers and the writers can then revise. Through this procedure, the papers get a rough screening. When the teacher reads the rewritten papers, his time is more profitably used. It takes a long time for a teacher to read a set of papers and to write searching and helpful comments on each. Only

serious efforts are worthy of the teacher's time and work. An initial screening and rewriting is some assurance that the compositions are results of some seriousness of effort. Procedures for conducting peer-group evaluation are described later in this chapter.

3. The writing of comments on the student's composition is a practical means for meeting his unique requirements. Although time consuming, that procedure does enable the teacher or other evaluator to identify shortcomings, bring these to the learner's attention, and prescribe corrective activities.

I have suggested that helping the student attain purpose in writing justifies all specific teaching of composition. Not only do the skills of the writer specify the desired learning—they also imply the needed activities. To determine what students need to learn, we examine their compositions. If the list of skills is right, the needs may be expressed as one or some combination of these. The learning activities may be inferred from the needs.

Distinguishing the principles of writing from the psychology of writers

Our inquiry shows that there are no rules for writing. Rather, a piece of writing comes about because a writer has exercised a limited set of skills. Because a composition is a consequence of the use of these skills, it is reasonable to call them the principles of writing. The principles, then, are not expressions of value or of virtue; they are the conditions for the existence of a discourse.

The chronological order in which writers write is quite another matter, as are their other habits of work. It is, therefore, dubious to expect to teach or learn how to write by asking the professional writer how to do it. Further, a competent practitioner of an art is not necessarily aware of the principles that guide his work. Usually, his use of the principles is unconscious.

Habits of work are not principles of construction. All writers, regardless of their individual habits, necessarily use the same basic principles of construction. Their use of these may occur in any chronological order and at varying degrees of awareness of just what these principles are.

An analogy with axmaking may clarify. One axmaker may begin by shaping the handle, another by making a wedge out of a block of steel, and still another by drilling a hole in a block of steel. But the same principles of construction, consciously or unconsciously, guide the work of all. The distinction being discussed suggests that each student be encouraged to find a way of working that he finds comfortable, and that the instruction emphasize the principles rather than a set of working habits.

Clarifying the process of writing[2]

Because the ideas discussed in the foregoing section suggest that much practice and opinion are at variance with the principles of writing, further clarification is required. Typically, the teaching of composition is conceived as a process of guiding the student toward what he should be doing first, second, third, and so on. By teaching a particular order of work, the teacher claims to be teaching the process of writing. Sometimes the process of writing is said to fall into phases, such as pre-writing, writing, and post-writing. However widely accepted, such views rest on a confusion between what anyone does as a writer and what anyone does as a person. The following discussion may clarify.

On the assumption that a composition is a whole consisting of parts, the construction of the parts that constitute the whole must define the task and the process of writing. The writer as a person may incubate ideas, prepare an outline, gather material, and sharpen pencils; all such activities are what someone does—not as a writer, but as a person. The reason is that activities that are external to the construction of the parts are not acts of writing but general human actions, and such actions are only accidentally related to a writing process.

This would seem evident when we realize that, while writing, different people perform different activities that are external to the construction of the parts, and the same person performs different external activities with respect to different discourses. Put another way, the making of the parts explains what the writing process must be. All other activities, therefore, are not indispensable to the production of a discourse and, consequently, cannot be an aspect of the process itself.

To clarify further, let us refer again to the axmaking trade. A certain axmaker may say that he can't do his work unless he takes time to think about what he has to do, arranges his tools, and smokes a corncob pipe. The process of axmaking, however, consists only of constructing the parts that constitute the whole, and that is all and only what he does as *axmaker*. These other activities are what he does as an individual and are only accidentally related to the making of axes. Because an ax can be made unaccompanied by the external activities, that establishes the accidental relationship.

In this view, there is a sense in which the term "writing process" is misleading. Each discourse is a different whole consisting of differences in parts. These differences in parts include those of representation of the author, details, and the rest. To speak of a single writing process is misleading in the sense that the processes necessarily differ according to the parts constructed. Moreover, different kinds of writing imply different processes of construction. Experience as well as logic justifies this contention. Poems, plays, and stories differ in kind. A writer of good fiction is not necessarily a writer of good plays, as the example of Henry James shows.

A process must have a beginning, an order, and an end. The beginning is not necessarily what the writer as a person does first. Rather, the beginning is whenever the first functioning part is constructed. Similarly, the order is not a chronological sequence of human actions, but the order of subordination of parts to whole. The process ends whenever a whole is formed and work on the parts is stopped or abandoned.

Finally, this conception offers further clarification about what this book has already said about comprehension. For example, Chapter 2 explains that the process of part-whole comprehension is that of inferring effects and explaining how the parts function to produce these. Other activities of the reader cannot, therefore, be part of this particular comprehension process. The analysis of ideas offers a different emphasis in comprehension. It follows that the processes of both comprehension and composition are to be discovered not by examining the overt activities of people, but by identifying the principles by which discourses are constructed.

Suggested learning activities

The accompanying syllabus briefly presents learning activities, all related to the construction of parts. The criteria for selecting learning activities that appear in the section "Justifying learning activities" in Chapter 1 are useful for selecting or devising others.

A syllabus of suggested learning activities

Learning activities refer to what the student is to do and usually imply the work of the teacher. The activities listed in the syllabus, it is important to note, are not a sequence for teaching, but an inventory from which selection may be made as the need arises.

1. Skills of purpose.
    1.1. *Identify a purpose for the composition.* (Introductory note: The specific, systematic teaching of composition should build upon work with part-whole comprehension. If students have acquired the learning at which the following activity is aimed, the activity is not necessary. But review may well be in order. The first activity aims at the student's distinguishing the purpose of a made thing from that thing itself. A composition is a made thing whose purpose is not the composition itself, but its intended effects. The ability to draw distinctions between the ends and means of made things in general is related to a proper conception of the ends and means of composition

in particular.) The teacher may review the purpose-of-a-car business in the section "Part-whole comprehension" in Chapter 2. After suggesting to the class that a composition, like a car, chair, or telephone, is a made thing, ask what the purpose of that made thing is. Arrive at the conclusion that its purpose is to produce effects upon readers—to inform, to persuade or influence, to entertain, to arouse within them some kind of emotion, or to produce within readers some combination of these effects or others. Ask students to:

1.11. Explain why purposes are not parts yet determine what the parts must be. Refer to simple objects such as hammers, saws, and tables.

1.12. Read an example of expository prose and state its intended effects upon readers. (They should justify their responses by explicit references to the text of the selection.)

1.13. Read a short, one-page composition written by a student in another class; on the reverse side of the paper is the writer's statement of purpose. Infer the writer's purpose, then check to see if the students' inferences agree with the purpose stated by the writer.

1.14. Read examples of student themes (dittoed from the teacher's file) and identify those which show no clear-cut purpose and those which do. Identify the purpose in the latter.

1.15. Compare two editorials from two newspapers that discuss the same issue, but with differing or opposing viewpoints. Identify the purpose of each.

1.16. Compile a list of items that might be found in a composition written to persuade the reader to vote for a particular candidate.

1.2. *Identify the intended reader(s) and make assumptions about him that affect what is written.* Ask students to:

1.21. List the characteristics of an audience of middle-

aged women which should be taken into con-
sideration when discussing narcotics.

1.22. Distinguish the characteristics of an audience
of their friends compared to an audience of
their teachers.

1.23. Distinguish two different age groups, describe
those characteristics which differentiate the two
groups; such differences would affect how one
writes about a given topic for each group.

1.24. Read or listen to a group of paragraphs written
by students. Infer the audience each seems to
be addressing. Identify the clues that justify
those inferences.

1.25. Read two articles—one from a children's magazine and one from a "good" adult magazine.
Contrast the articles as to subject and vocabulary. Explain adaptation of article to audience.

1.26. Rewrite a newspaper article so that it would
suit a younger audience, perhaps third graders.

1.27. Adapt an article on Pop Art or some other
subject to interest at least one audience
different from the one at which it is aimed.

1.28. Ask students to bring in copies of advertisements for Volkswagens and for Cadillacs.
Discuss in class the differences in the intended
readers, and the differences in techniques for
affecting those readers.

2. *Skills of product*

2.1. *Identify what is to be argued or explained:* Ask
students to:

2.11. Read pieces of writing each of which has a
different purpose. Identify what, essentially, is
being argued or explained in each. Relate these
means to effects.

2.12. Write a beginning topic sentence for an essay
they would like to write. Explain clearly the
reader at whom the essay is aimed, the intended
purpose or the effects sought, the topic (cats,

girls, boys, politics) and the specific explanation or argument that is best suited to the intended essay.

2.13. Identify a community situation and plan to respond to it in writing. An example: Your neighborhood has no playground or swimming pool. Some people think that these should be installed in a vacant lot; others are fighting the project. Plan to write a letter to the editor of the local newspaper in which you express your view. State your purpose and what you will argue or explain.

2.2. *Convey a representation of the author and his attitudes toward the audience, the topic, and himself.* Ask students to:

2.21. Give examples of what roles they play— brother, sister, son, daughter, student, employee, and so on. Relate the playing of roles to the act of writing a composition, specifically to the importance of the role or representation of the author in achieving desired effects.

2.22. List ways a reader can determine how the writer represents himself to his reader—for example, a typical student, an outraged citizen, a solid citizen, one who plays it dumb. Infer these roles of the writer from letters-to-the-editor or from some similar source.

2.23. Read several examples of expository prose and discuss each author's role and his purpose for assuming that role.

2.24. Identify a convincing role for a writer if he were arguing that skiing (or motorcycling or drag-car racing) is dangerous.

2.25. Determine for a specific topic and purpose the appropriate role for the writer to assume.

2.26. Read the beginning page or so of any textbook at hand. Identify the attitude that the author takes toward his audience, his topic, and himself. Typically, the writer of a textbook attempts to convey the impression that he is an expert on his topic, that he takes his topic seriously, and that he is sympathetic and helpful toward his readers. How do such matters function to produce the desired effect or combination of effects?

2.27. Adapt 2.26 above to any essay or article that the students think is good. (Each student may select his own selection from any appropriate source.)

2.3. *Present thoughts, facts, ideas, arguments, examples, and so on that are suited to purpose and reader.* Ask students to:

2.31. Infer from a given article where and how the author gathered his materials. List possible sources the writer might use in obtaining information for certain topics (Working at the Check-out Counter, Confronting a Problem).

2.32. Form groups within the class. Each group is to select a topic and purpose. The students work together to make a list of anecdotes, facts, ideas or thoughts that could be used for the topic and purpose chosen by the group. After the list is completed, each student chooses the five items that he believes are best suited to the topic and purpose of his group. He must justify his choice.

2.33. Assume "to amuse" as a purpose for writing, and collect the most entertaining anecdotes the students hear around the school all this week. Feel free to "improve" on the stories.

2.4. *Organize the details into a sequence.* Ask students to:

2.41. Read a piece of explanatory or argumentative prose that they think is good. Identify the order used by the author. Explain why that order is suited to the purpose.

2.42. Read two or more compositions on the same subject. Compare and contrast the kinds of order used by each writer. Relate order to purpose.

2.43. Suggest as many details as possible for a given topic and purpose, then discuss appropriate methods of organization and needs for limiting or adding details.

2.44. State and defend a plan of organization for a given topic and purpose. A topic may be "Automobile Salesrooms Should (or Should Not) Be Open on Sundays," and the purpose may be to persuade.

2.45. Explain what impressions the following statement would produce upon almost any reader: "I shall state my reasons, not in any particular order, but just as they come to mind."

2.5. *Emphasize certain of the details or sets of details.* Ask students to:

2.51. Identify the emphasis in any example of exposition or argument. Explain the relation between emphasis and effects.

2.52. Explain the emphasis in this phrase: "A man living in France and burdened with trouble." (Lead them to see that approximately equal space is allotted to "man," "France," and "trouble," yet "man" is the most fully presented to the reader. The reason is that "France" and "trouble" modify "man." Thus, not only is emphasis achieved through relative amount of space, but also through syntactic relationships.)

2.6. *Select from the resources of the language appropriate words, sentence patterns, and varieties of usage.* Ask students to:

2.61. Read explanations of a process or a term as written on various levels, each for a particular audience. Note choice of words and sentence structure for different kinds of readers. Explain these differences. For example: respiration, planet, missile, as defined and illustrated in: (a) elementary texts; (b) junior high level tests;

(c) *Encyclopedia Britannica;* (d) college or technical level texts.

2.62. Explain differences between an article on today's space program written in *Scientific American* and an article on that topic written in *Time*. List the differences in language, paying particular attention to vocabulary and length and complexity of sentences.

2.63. Read two articles on the same subject, one in a publication for second-graders and another in a publication for adults. Ask the students to explain and justify differences in vocabulary and length of sentences.

2.64. Explain the ways a writer can adapt his language to fit his audience, his topic, and his purpose (i.e., lengths of sentences; word choice— erudite or common, formal or colloquial.

2.65. Compare and contrast the language advertising the same product in *The New Yorker* and *Reader's Digest*.

2.66. Listen to someone read an anonymous essay whose main fault is unfortunate sentence structure, and through discussion, identify the faults. The students may discuss the manip- ulating of words and sentences so that a revised essay results. The revised version should be clearer and more pleasing when read both silently and orally. Individual practice may follow using other essays, including each student's own.

2.7. *Write in a style that is appropriate to writing (rather than speech) and to the literary conventions expected in essays, articles, or other kinds of writing.* Ask students to:

2.71. Explain various styles and conventions using well-written examples of expository prose. Distinguish personal essays from factual articles by indicating the kinds of sentence patterns and choices of words each tends to employ.

For example: Compare and contrast "straight reporting" of news items to personal essays. Use particular writings and distinguish the language and effects of each.

2.72. Compare the writing styles of *Reader's Digest* with those used in the *Saturday Review* and the *Atlantic,* following the procedure described in 2.71 above.

2.73. Read a written transcription of speech and suggest ways in which the language may be changed in order to be appropriate to writing. For example, the quotation that follows is a transcription of a tape recording. A transcription of speech is a form of discourse that is different from that expected of writing. Here Elliott Roosevelt describes orally the night his father, Franklin D. Roosevelt, was elected President. Read the transcription and then translate it into the discourse of writing.

On election night in 1932 they had the ticker tape and the telephone set up in one room, and all the operators and the principal workers were gathered around that room. For a long period of time Father stayed out of the room, but as the returns started to really come in, and it became apparent that he was moving ahead in the early stages, he just couldn't resist it. He came into the room, and then he set up charts and he followed each state, each county in the United States, with the greatest of interest, and he kept cautioning all of the people around: "Now, don't get excited, this can change." But it didn't change, so after a while, I'd say about midnight or 12:30 he felt that the election was really won, and of course, that called for a lot of backslapping and a great deal of pleasant celebrating, and I think he stayed up until about three o'clock that night. When he went to bed, he was completely sure that he had won the election because by that time most of the major cities in California, which were the last ones to be heard from, had come in.[3]

2.8. *Follow the conventions of the writing system.*
Prefatory note: "Conventions of the writing system"
refers to such matters as spelling, punctuation,
paragraphing, and the like. These belong only to
writing, not to speech.

2.81. A word of warning must preface descriptions
of learning activities. It is common practice
to teach such units of study as the comma, the
question mark, and spelling. That kind of
activity, however, is usually an escape from
the teaching of composition: The only reason
for learning to spell, capitalize, and punctuate
is the use of those skills in writing. To avoid
teaching what is not needed and what is easily
forgotten, I suggest that the conventions of the
writing system, like the other aspects of
composition, be taught as the need arises.
If students are confused by such matters as
when to capitalize, when to insert a comma,
when to insert a semicolon, and when not to,
the teacher may provide the needed instruction
by following these steps:

a. Identify the source of difficulty. For example,
perhaps the students don't know when to
capitalize.

b. Translate the source of difficulty into a statement of one or more specific skills, such that
the learning of these skills is likely to result
in the needed improvement. For example.
"Distinguish written words that conventionally begin with capitals from those that
do not."

c. Provide learning activities for the skills to be
learned. For example, composition texts,
workbooks, and handbooks on usage typically provide such exercises.

d. Note the performance of the skills on
subsequent compositions. Point out diffi-

culties that remain; praise acceptable
performance.

2.82. Ask students to read an anonymous paper that
contains faults in the conventions of the writing
system. They may read such a paper by means
of the overhead projector or by duplicated
copies. First, discuss the probable responses of
the intended reader to the faults. Second, the
teacher might explain that not much logic or
necessity justifies the existence of some (not
all) of the conventions. For example, the
distinction between capital letter and "small"
letter is actually unnecessary and therefore
wasteful. Telegrams are typed in capitals, as is
much of the typed material of the United States
Navy, and there is no loss of clarity. But
although such matters can be shown to be
useless on logical grounds, violations of these
conventional expectations produce adverse
effects on the conventionally educated reader.

2.83. Ask students to grade compositions of peers.
Indicate needed revisions with respect to the
conventions of the writing system along with
other needed revisions. These provide guidance
for revising and rewriting. A detailed discussion
of this activity appears later in this chapter.

Revising and rewriting

It is just about impossible for even highly gifted writers
to produce an acceptable first draft. For this reason, revising
and rewriting ought to be an objective even though these
are not themselves the principles of writing. Secondary-school
students probably don't revise as much as they should because their teachers are overloaded.

This chapter discusses revising and rewriting as well as
a procedure whereby the teacher's paper-reading burden may
be reduced through students' suggesting revisions for each
other's writing. In addition, as preparation for the study of

the procedures just mentioned, I suggest such classroom activities as asking students to:

Explain the slogan, "Good writing is not written but rewritten."

Read a sequence of badly-written sentences from an anonymous student's paper. The paper may be duplicated or written on the board or projected on the overhead. Suggest revisions.

Read each other's papers before giving these to the teacher. Suggest revisions. Discuss these with the writers, who would then revise and rewrite before submitting them to the teacher.

As mentioned, more systematic evaluative procedures appear later in this chapter.

With the skills of writing specified and some related learning activities presented, I turn now to a discussion of the assignment and the more systematic evaluation of writing.

The assignment of writing

Chapter 1 explains why behavior and content must comprise objectives. The *content* for composition is any aspect of the universe within the student's direct or vicarious experience; the principles of writing specify the behavioral aspect. Although topics available for composition must be drawn from the student's experience, he is likely to have favorable attitudes toward his writing if he is genuinely concerned about his topic—more specifically, if he has (or can be led to have) ideas, feeling, and convictions about it so strong that he wants to give them expression.

The day-to-day work with students offers abundant opportunity to identify and stimulate such concerns. Here are some kinds of class discussions from which we may identify appropriate topics: the interpretations of a literary work, social problems of the adolescent, and controversial issues of the local, national, or world community. To put it briefly, any subject that arouses ideas and feelings may be formulated into a topic for writing.

For example, there was a public controversy in the neighborhood of a Chicago high school about automobile salesrooms being open on Sundays. Discussion in class as well as the concern of the wider community aroused a variety of opinion. Compositions on the topic, therefore, were assigned. The papers written were mainly of two kinds—one urged the acceptance of one or another viewpoint; the other surveyed opinion and arrived at conclusions.

A local journalistic know-it-all provided another occasion for controversy. In his newspaper column, he made these observations: During the stock-market crash of 1929, a number of prominent businessmen who lost their fortunes committed suicide. Apparently these men couldn't handle failure. In every human life, however, some failure is inevitable. It is necessary, therefore, that people learn how to deal with failure when they meet it. To teach people to handle failure, our columnist wrote, schools should upon occasion purposely fail students.

The classroom discussion of that statement aroused intense feeling. All writing that resulted said essentially the same thing. But motivation was high, and that is a desirable condition under which to teach and learn writing or anything else.

A student's commitment to a topic cannot be aroused merely because it is current, controversial, and important. Essays on the latest Presidential campaign can be at least as mechanically written as those on "My Summer Vacation." Nor will lists of 1,000 catchy topics for written composition necessarily do the job. The best choices come from what the teacher observes to be his students' genuine concerns.

To put it briefly, we foster learning by exploiting the interests and convictions of students. Under some conditions a literary or linguistic problem may exploit such interest. Typically, however, their real interests and convictions are neither literary nor linguistic. Arnold Bennet referred to the small minority who are devoted to literature as "the passionate few."

Yet in journals for English teachers, some authors urge that writing be limited to literary topics because of an assumption that literature is the "soul" or the "center" of the English curriculum. Using a similar line of reasoning, other authors claim that the "soul" or the "center" is language or linguistics, which, according to their view, should provide the subjects for composition.

I hold, however, that neither of these latter views can be sustained. English as a school subject is not a unified discipline but an accident of history.

Algebra may be thought of as a unified discipline with distinctive problems and methods of inquiry. English, however, is similar to social studies: the two fields consist of a number of separate subjects. History, geography, and economics are subjects or disciplines included within the field of the social studies. Composition, language, and literature are the subjects traditional to English. It is arguable whether there can be a "soul" or "center" to such a miscellany. This brief aside on the English curriculum leads to the conclusion that the purpose for selecting topics for composition is not to foster a dubious unity, but to help students write.

The use of lively topics need not imply that anything goes. All too often we find students who want to set everyone straight on juvenile delinquency, the dropout, the drug problem, and so on. No teacher need apologize for refusing to read immature comment on social issues so complicated that there are no recognized authorities on them. Nor need a teacher feel that he is suppressive if he finds certain topics aversive or exasperating and lets his students know it. The world is full of a number of things, and even if a few topics are forbidden the student has a limitless number from which to choose. Teachers who suppress their exasperations are not really honest with their students, and students feel more at ease when their teachers level with them.

The selection of topics is only one aspect of assigning writing. Another is the selection of purpose. Although a writer, whether novice or professional, may want to write on a particular subject, he may not know when he begins just what he intends to say or what effects he is after. Such matters may become clear to him only toward the end of his task. There are occasions, however, when the only reason for writing is to produce certain effects upon certain readers.

Everyday examples include letters, notes, and memoranda. We may say, then, that the job of writing and the utilitarian demands of the world suggest that assignments include those in which sometimes the student writes for particular purposes and at other times he arrives at purposes by himself.

The discussion just concluded implies the following criteria for the assignment of writing:

1. The content of the subject must be within the learner's experience or easily accessible to him.
2. The learner must have some ideas, feelings, or convictions about the content or subject.
3. Both intended reader and the effects that the writing is designed to have upon him must be conceived in the mind of the writer at some time before, during, or after the writing. The assignment must either specify the intended reader and effects to be produced upon him or should require the student to arrive at those decisions for himself.
4. (Optional.) The content or subject should not repel the teacher who has to read and evaluate the writing. If a teacher finds particular topics distasteful, he should without apology identify these topics and put them on the *verboten* list.

The evaluation of writing

A piece of writing is evaluated by determining the extent to which its purposes are likely to be achieved. As explained in Chapter 3, the actual achievement of purpose is not a criterion of assessment.

We have assumed throughout that a piece of writing is successful to the extent that the writer has properly used the skills of writing. Faults in a composition, therefore, may be explained as faults in the writer's practice of one or some combination of those skills. Thus, proper criteria for evaluating compositions draw the attention of the teacher or other evaluator and student to the skills needing more work. In the accompanying outline, I cite and explain these criteria.

CRITERIA FOR EVALUATING WRITTEN COMPOSITIONS

The skills of writing appear below in a form convenient for evaluating compositions. In a particular composition, its parts are judged by their function in producing intended effects upon the intended reader. Therefore, any given part cannot be judged as good, bad, or indifferent in itself.

1. *Purpose* (intended effects).
    1.1. Are the effects to be produced upon the reader inferrable?
    1.2. Are the characteristics assumed of the perceived reader inferrable?
2. *Form* (main argument, explanation, description, justification, and so on). Is there an ascertainable main argument or explanation that is properly related to the purpose?
3. *Nonverbal parts.*
    3.1. Representation of author and attitudes conveyed.
        3.11. Is the author's representation of himself consistent and suited to the purpose?
        3.12. Are the attitudes (expressed or implied) toward the author himself, his topic, and his reader suited to the purpose?
    3.2. Detail and organization.
        3.21. Is the selection of details appropriate to the purpose?
        3.22. Are the details arranged in a sequence on some rational or psychological basis?
    3.3. Emphasis.
        3.31. Are the degrees of emphasis upon details and sections suited to the purpose?
        3.32. If there is equal emphasis, is it justified?
4. *Verbal part or language.*
    4.1. Are vocabulary, sentence structure, and varieties of usage appropriate? (Is he using the right words and sentences?)

4.2. Is the style one that is expected of writing rather than one expected of speech? (Does the writing sound like writing and not like speech?)

4.3. Is the style appropriate to the literary genre, such as essay and article, in which the selection is written? (If it's an essay does it sound like one and not like a newspaper report of a baseball game?)

4.4. Are conventions of the writing system followed?

4.5. Are any departures from these or from any other conventions justified?

To illustrate the use of the criteria, they will be applied to the composition that follows. Here is the assignment to which the composition is a response: "Your community has a junior and a senior high school. The senior high has a swimming pool, but the junior high does not. There is a movement among some members of the community to provide the junior high with a swimming pool. Others in the community are against the project. Write a letter to the editor of the community newspaper in which you attempt to persuade a typical reader of that newspaper to accept your point of view."

Dear Sir:

1	There is a swimming pool in the senior high school.	1
2	The junior high unfortunately does not, and many leading	2
3	citizens in the community and the students of the junior	3
4	high would like to have one built. I think a swimming	4
5	pool in the junior high would be very beneficial. The	5
6	students would not have to wait until they are in high	6
7	school to learn how to swim. The high school must	7
8	serve the entire school district and when the pool is	8
9	open for public swimming it becomes overcrowded. Swim-	9
10	ming competition is reduced because there is only one	10
11	pool. It is not possible to have swimming teams comparable	11
12	with other schools if the swim team's practice sessions	12
13	are few because of an overcrowded pool. With a pool in	13
14	the junior high, there could be swimming classes In the	14
15	junior high while the swim team practices in the senior	15
16	high. There would be a very slight raise in taxes but	16
17	the need is great and the gain in prestige our schools	17
18	would gain is enormous.	18

Susan Johnsen
Glens Falls Junior High School
Ninth Grade

James H. Sledd has evaluated this piece of writing. His comments and a rewriting that results from his comments follow. The comments, it should be noted, exemplify the use of the criteria just cited. These make explicit a coherent relationship among effects, main argument, and the non-verbal and verbal parts. Notice, too, that the relationship among order, emphasis, and language is this student's main problem.

Line 2: Doesn't what? Say *has no pool.*

Lines 2, 3: Reverse the order of *leading citizens and students,* so that you won't seem anticlimactic.

Line 4: Begin a new paragraph.

Change *think* to *agree that,* for a better transition from Paragraph 1.

Introduce the idea of prestige here, not in your last sentence. Placed in the topic sentence of your second paragraph, the idea of prestige will prepare for your argument about the success of the swimming team.

Add a phrase like *for at least two reasons,* so as to make a clear transition from your judgment to the reasons which justify it.

Line 5: Number your arguments so as to give your probably hurried reader every assistance.

Line 8: Comma after *district* to separate two independent clauses joined by *and.*

Line 9: Delete the sentence beginning *Swimming competition.* You have the same idea, by implication, in the following sentence; and the repetition makes your letter wordy.

Line 11: Say *a good swimming team* (singular) and delete *comparable with other schools.* To begin with, the change makes your letter shorter; and besides, you can't logically compare a team to a school. You need the singular number because you have the singular in line 12.

Line 12: Delete *swim.* Everybody knows what team you're talking about, and anyway you wouldn't change from *swimming team* to *swim team* without any reason.

Line 14: For *in the junior high* substitute *there.*

Line 15: Delete *swim* again, and keep your tenses consistent by using *practiced* (past tense) to match *could.*

Last sentence: Begin a new paragraph, and rewrite. You've already used most of this last sentence in your revised paragraph 2, and you don't want to put too much emphasis on those rising taxes. So—*These benefits, in my opinion, would more than justify any slight rise in taxes.*

The letter is revised as follows.

Dear Sir:

There is a swimming pool in the senior high school. The junior high school unfortunately has no pool, and the students of the junior high and many leading citizens in the community would like to have one built.

I agree that a swimming pool in the junior high would be very beneficial and would give our school system great prestige, for at least two reasons. (1) Students would not have to wait until they are in high school to learn how to swim. (2) The high school pool must serve the entire school district, and when the pool is open for public swimming it becomes overcrowded. It is not possible to have a good swimming team if the team's practice sessions are few because of an overcrowded pool. With a pool in the junior high, there could be swimming classes there while the team practiced in the senior high.

These benefits, in my opinion, would more than justify any slight rise in taxes.

Susan Johnsen
Glens Falls Junior High School
Ninth Grade

The letter-to-the-editor we have been considering is the work of a good student. All too often, however, we are faced with something like this:

The principle reason I want to go to college is to extend my education. By doing this I will be assured of better job offerings.

College will give me a fuller adult life. When things happen in "the world of tomorrow" I will have a better background on the subject.[4]

We need no list of criteria or detailed comment for this performance. The problem here is to help the student decide who he is writing for, what effects he wishes to produce upon him, and which argument is suited to that purpose.

Helping students while relieving the teacher's paper-reading burden

As indicated, the teaching of composition requires careful reading and evaluating of compositions, followed by instruction and practice in the skills needing further work. This implies guidance of individuals. The task is detailed and time-consuming and there are no facile short cuts.

There are, however, at least three reasons to suppose that students may share the burden of evaluation: (1) research and experience show a consistent success of projects in which students help each other; (2) the work of testing agencies demonstrates high reliability in the evaluation of compositions when the raters of these are given instruction and practice in the use of evaluative criteria; and (3) the principles of writing imply comprehensive evaluative criteria, an example of which has been presented.

Such reasons justify efforts to teach students how to evaluate compositions. A suggested procedure follows:

1. Begin after students have had specific instruction in both part-whole comprehension and in written composition.
2. Distribute copies of a form for evaluating composition. Use the one in this chapter, a revision of it, or some other. Explain to the class that this form guides the marking of papers.
3. Display or distribute copies of a short, anonymous composition and explain the use of the criteria in evaluating it.
4. Distribute copies of another short, anonymous composition and the evaluative criteria, which are the same for all papers. Conduct a discussion on the use of the criteria. The criteria imply the questions to be asked and are grounds for reaching consensus. Teach until most students acquire facility.

5. Assign a composition for students and reward those writing the four or five best compositions by naming them Evaluators.
6. Assign another composition to be evaluated by the class. Divide the class into an appropriate number of evaluation groups. Name an Evaluator to lead each group. Within each group, students evaluate each other's papers. The Evaluator guides, supervises, checks, and specifically handles the papers of the weakest. In that way, avoid the situation in which the weaker evaluates the work of the stronger. As a result of these efforts, students revise and rewrite.

Pitfalls

The main violations of the principles takes the form of escape from teaching composition: For example, teaching is based on the assumption that writing is a chronologically ordered process. Thus, the principles receive less emphasis than matters external and accidental to the principles. In another degradation, attention to grammar and usage takes on an undue dominance: purpose, whole, and nonverbal parts are neglected, although these determine what the language ought to be. The result is a dubious usefulness and certainly the misteaching of language as the verbal part that functions within the whole.

In another debasement, the teacher overcorrects a lively and spontaneous paper, transforming it into something hyper-correct but lifeless. Still another is a practice that assumes that there can be a good paper without reference to effects and intended reader. Under this conception, the teacher's opinions or his unverifiable value judgments are the only criteria for discussion and evaluation.

Summary

1. The basic principle for guiding the writing of a composition is that the piece of writing, including all of its parts, is a means for producing effects upon readers.

2. One is likely to produce these effects to the extent that he exercises the operational principles of writing. These principles are the same for all writers, whether beginner or professional.

3. The teaching of written composition is properly aimed toward a single objective, which may be stated, "Write explanatory and argumentative prose that is likely to achieve its purpose." A complete inventory of the skills of writing is the set of intermediate objectives for teaching to write.

4. Any order in which the skills are listed is not an order of instruction, but simply an inventory. Needs of learners determine which of the skills or which combinations of these require instruction.

5. There is no logical or empirical reason for curriculum plans that are based on the assumption that certain skills or certain lengths of writing belong to certain years of schooling.

6. The content for writing is the learner's direct and vicarious experience, and the skills are the operational principles. A minimal set of materials for teaching and learning to write, then, is a dictionary, a handbook of usage, some examples of well-written explanatory and argumentative prose, and, perhaps, an inventory of the skills of a writer.

7. A teacher of composition is a person who helps his students write to achieve a purpose. Concerns about bringing students "up to grade," about covering materials in text-books and curriculum guides, about working through an externally imposed sequence of instruction, are needless worries once the teacher understands that the aim is to improve each student's performance.

8. A procedure for teaching the writing skills is thorough reading. Conscious knowledge of how to write implies an ability to criticize the writing of others. Students can be taught to use the evaluative criteria for criticizing the writing of their peers and to suggest revisions. That procedure eases the paper-reading burden of teachers and helps students improve their writing.

9. The principles of writing are means for the rational teaching and discussion of a complicated skill. This implies

reasoned and reasonable grounds for the comments of teachers. The following comment is vague and evasive: "I marked your composition down because I don't like the way you ended it." Here, for example, is a clear and helpful evaluative comment: "The reader your composition is aimed at is not likely to know what 'existentialism' means."

10. There are no rules for composition. There is a limited set of operational principles. Through the use of these principles or skills the writer necessarily does his work. So does the teacher of writing.

11. This view of writing makes it convenient to clarify certain widely used rhetorical terms. Some examples:

coherence	Divisions related by logical or psychological principles.
conciseness	Economy of means in producing effects.
emphasis	Varying or equal levels of intensity among the parts and divisions suited to the producing of effects.
sequence	Order of presentation as a means for producing effects.
transition	Devices used to convince the reader that one division leads logically to another.
unity	A set of mutually supporting effects caused by proper construction.

The student-writer may perform these skills in whatever order he chooses. He may or he may not be aware of what these skills are or of the relationship among them. But having decided to produce an explanation or argument in writing he is consciously or unconsciously committed to certain consequences. Not only is he bound to the skills of writing, he is also bound to do what can feasibly be done with language. For example, C. S. Lewis has noted that "Those who think they are testing a boy's 'elementary' command of English by asking him to describe in words how one ties one's tie or what a pair of scissors is like, are far astray. For precisely what language can hardly do at all, and never does well, is to inform us about complex physical shapes and movements."[5]

Within these bounds the writer is free to use his firsthand or vicarious experiences for seeking to affect whom he will for whatever ends he may consciously or unconsciously select.

Exercises

Exercise 1

Follow the procedures illustrated in the foregoing pages with respect to any one or any number of the following pieces of actual, unedited student writing. For each composition, first number the lines in the composition to be evaluated, as shown on the student's letter to the editor. Then, type specific comments on a separate piece of paper; refer to particular words, phrases, sentences, and so on, and give reasons for those comments. Follow Sledd's example given earlier in this chapter. Finally, type a copy of the composition as you would have it revised—that is, prepare a rewritten composition in which the changes you suggest are incorporated. An example is the rewriting of the student's letter to the editor.

My Important Traits

Very often, a person's traits determine what occupation he is going to have in life. Many of Gordon Parks' interests influenced his choice of jobs as a life's work. Just as his interests influenced him, my interests will influence my choice.

I feel that three of my most important traits are my perseverance, my interest in people and my "intelligence." Hastily I explain that what I mean by "intelligence" is my ability, want, and drive to know, to find out about my environment. You really can not do much without that. Corelated with that is my perseverance—my drive, the motivation and force that makes me want to do something. That is important, because in order to succeed in anything you must be compelled to strive to do well in it. Also, my interest in people is important, because if I pick an occupation such as doctor, lawyer (or almost any occupation, because most deal with people) I would find that such an interest would greatly help me along in my work. All these interests are important.

Also, I might find useful my interests in Science, photography, music and creative writing (such as poetry . . .). I would find my interests in science necessary if I were to become a doctor. I would probably use photography as a hobby. I might write books also on the side, as an occupation.

All these interests would find place in influencing my choice for an occupation for life.

Our Campfire

As I sat around the campfire one night I watched the tongues of fire lick my hot-dog which I held on the end of a green stick. It was chilly that night and I felt the warmth of the fire in my face. My dog slept peacefuly next to me. As I sat there roasting my hot-dog, the wind whistled through the trees. I took the hot-dog out of the fire, walked to my tent and took out a bun. As I walked back eating a bun I smelled marshmallows roasting. Rob, my tent-mate sat eating a marshmallow. I joined in. The fire shifted directions as I had eaten my fill. I started carving on a piece of wood. "Funny, I thought, I don't even know what I making." After a while I glanced at my watch. It read 11:40. "We ought to be hitting the sack pretty soon." I said to Rob. "Yeah." agreed Rob. Just then the fire died down. The moon went behind the trees and the coals of the fire glowed bright orange as I crept into my dark tent.

The Final Exams

. . . the teacher hands the exam to the student. The boy says in a small and wistful tone:

"Do I have to?" The teacher glares at him. Now the teacher goes to the person behind him. The boy revieces the paper and and gulps. He studies the paper and looks pale and then notices the teacher staring at him. "Obviusly you didn't study!" the teacher thunders. "Oh I did," "But not this." the student says shakily. The boy goes back to studying the paper. Now the eighth grade suddenly is let out in the halk. A loud roar of talking begins. The teacher runs to the door, grumbles, and quickly closes the door; too quickly. He then slams it with a loud bang. One student looks up "Cheat!" the teacher roars. "Oh no, not again!" the student thinks nervously. The teacher-aid presumes the teacher's job—handing out final exams.

Exercise 2.

Obtain a copy of a typical composition of 250 words or so. Note how long it takes you to evaluate it carefully and conscientiously and to write helpful comments on it. Multiply the time spent by the number of students in composition taught by one teacher in your community. Add to that figure the number of hours such a teacher spends in teaching and in performing other duties of the school that may be done during or beyond the school day. What are the total number of hours? What does this imply for the career of English teaching, for the teaching of composition, and for the evaluation of writing?

Notes

1. As a whole, this chapter is a logical consequence of the principles of construction and of evaluation discussed in the three preceding chapters. Notes to those chapters, therefore, apply to this one.

2. The argument incorporated into this section is taken from Elder Olson, "The Poetic Process," *Critical Inquiry*, 2, No. 1 (Autumn 1975), 69–74. In this article the principles expounded apply equally to any form or kind of oral or written discourse whatsoever.

3. "F.D.R.: As We Remember Him." *The Saturday Evening Post*, 238 (April 10, 1965), 38.

4. Royal J. Morsey, *Improving English Instruction* (2nd ed.; Boston: Allyn and Bacon, 1969), p. 246.

5. C. S. Lewis, *Studies in Words* (Cambridge: Cambridge University Press, 1960), p. 313.

CHAPTER 6

FUNDAMENTALS FOR THE TEACHING OF LITERATURE

*The chapter discusses goals for the teaching of litera-
ture, suggests activities for introducing the study, and describes some terms, distinctions and activities for teaching
basic literary comprehension.*

Beginning with a discussion of reading for fun, this chapter
next gives a brief explanation of some distinctions that are
fundamental to literary study. In the two chapters that follow,
these ideas are developed further with respect to the forms
of literature: poetry, drama, and fiction.

Reading for fun

A program in literature may well begin by inculcating or
sustaining the habit of reading books, magazines, and newspapers for sheer enjoyment. It is easy to foster this habit
because everyone is interested in human actions and the
things of this world. From such a basis of enjoyment, we may
develop readers of literature.

Both research and everyday experience suggest that people
read what they find accessible and readable. A work is
readable when the student finds it interesting and unburden-
some to read. Therefore, the reading habit may be encouraged
by classrooms supplied with readable materials and by visits
to the school or public library.

A teacher may help his students identify readable books
by holding a class discussion on personal interests in reading,

thereby arousing interest as well as bringing particular titles to the attention of the class. There are other sources of titles as well: teachers in the same or in a similar community; school and public librarians, particularly those specializing in books for adolescents; college or university specialists in books for younger readers; and the book lists compiled by the American Library Association and by the National Council of Teachers of English.

The NCTE, for example, sponsors the compilation and dissemination of *Books for You,* an annotated list for senior high school, and *Your Reading,* an annotated list for junior high. Both are revised periodically.

The free-reading period is a desirable use of the school's time, particularly in disadvantaged communities. A discussion of this appears in the section of Chapter 2 in which I treat the teaching of comprehension to the reluctant reader. Ideally, the free-reading period encourages each student to read or to continue a book that he will feel compelled to finish on his own.

A related activity is a free-wheeling discussion of books read and being read. This is an opportunity for students to express their reactions, which become suggestions about what to read and what to avoid. Here we use the power of the group to stimulate reading.

That vexed topic, the book report, requires some comment. I suggest that free reading be treated as an enjoyable activity both inside and outside the school, that no grades be given for it, and that it be kept low-keyed and unpressured. The time of the teacher is better spent helping to match students and books than in assigning and evaluating book reports.

When students look upon reading as a source of satisfaction, they are ready to be taught literary comprehension in systematic fashion. The intelligent conduct of such instruction requires that the teacher understand a few basic ideas, which we will now consider.

Comprehension and appreciation

There is no warrant for the popular opinion that close analysis kills appreciation. The earlier chapters on the comprehension of argument show that reading well means close and unwavering attention to what is read. So it is with imaginative literature. Good poems, plays, and fiction are at least as demanding as good expository prose.

Although an important aim of literary study is pleasure, we miss the point if close analysis is not a means to increased appreciation. Years ago, John Dewey explained the relationship between such emotional or affective outcomes as interests and appreciation, on the one hand, and the cognitive, on the other: "[I believe that] if we can only secure right habits of action and thought, with reference to the good, the true, and the beautiful, the emotions will for the most part take care of themselves."[1] On the assumption that certain skills of comprehension and related ideas are examples of these "right habits of action and thought," this book goes on to suggest what at least some of these are and what they imply for teaching.

Works of literature as primary sources

The study of literature at any level is unique in its dependence upon primary sources. It is possible (whether desirable or not) to teach history through such secondary sources as expository and discursive textbooks whose level of comprehension may be selected to correspond with the level of intelligence and literacy of the learners. But one can learn poetry only by learning to read and analyze particular poems.

Put differently, to learn poetry, a student must acquire the analytic and synthetic tasks of the literary critic (at whatever level of performance is suitable for him). The secondary-school student of history, however, is seldom expected to learn the tasks of the historian, only some results or conclusions of the historian's art.

Literary principles: Introductory note

Although literature offers aesthetic and moral contributions to a student's life, these arise from the systematic study of particular selections. Such study is more complicated and fascinating than typical instruction in secondary schools would suggest.

In the rest of this chapter, I sketch out some of these fundamental ideas that give interest, coherence, and feasibility to the study of literature, even in classes of typical students in secondary schools. Further, I offer suggestions by which these ideas may be taught and learned. By doing this, I am not presenting a curriculum. Rather, I am attempting to identify and clarify some basic principles that the teacher may use in his planning, teaching, and evaluating. The ideas should be taught during the study of particular works and as the need arises. To exemplify with specific instances, I find it convenient to refer throughout to Whitman's "When I Heard the Learn'd Astronomer."

When I Heard the Learn'd Astronomer

When I heard the learn'd astronomer,
When the proofs, the figures, were ranged in columns
    before me,
When I was shown the charts and diagrams, to add,
    divide, and measure them,
When I sitting heard the astronomer where he lectured
    with much applause in the lecture room,
How soon unaccountable I became tired and sick,
Till rising and gliding out I wander'd off by myself,
In the mystical moist night-air, and from time to time,
Look'd up in perfect silence at the stars.

Walt Whitman

The literary audience and its responses to literature[2]

As the four preceding chapters indicate, arguments in expository prose are usually intended for a particular reader or group. Names of publications suggest the varying audiences to which such prose must be adapted—for example, *Reader's Digest, Fortune,* and the *Shaker High School Bison.*
With respect to literature, however, the audience is dif-

ferent. To think clearly about the comprehension of, and responses to, the better poems, plays, and fiction, teachers must have a clear idea of who the reader is. However high-flown the term, I refer to him as the "qualified reader." The term implies neither elitism nor snobbishness. In what follows, I explain why we need this distinction.

In our culture, good literature is not written for everyone in the sense that an ad on television is. Literary works of at least some distinction are intended for those who (1) get the literal sense of what is going on in such selections and (2) respond conventionally or appropriately or properly to good and bad, right and wrong, admirable and contemptible.

More specifically, the qualified reader will be outraged at acts of cruelty and senseless violence; he will pity undeserved misfortune; he will admire courage and integrity. He will not respond to acts of cruelty with sadistic joy nor to undeserved misfortune with lofty indifference. Moreover, he judges human actions properly and sympathetically. For instance, he knows that people differ in temperament, powers, and limitations, and that these matters must be taken into account in judging what people do, say, think, and feel.

A broad goal of literary study, we may therefore propose, is the making of qualified readers. In the sense that the qualified reader is intelligent and humane, such a goal, also, is shared by education generally. There are, of course, a number of other ways to express that objective.

To illustrate the responses of the qualified reader is to explain comprehension and intended effects. This may be demonstrated with a particular work without accounting for all aspects of comprehension. For example, after reading "When I Heard the Learn'd Astronomer," our idealized reader will feel a sympathetic pleasure as the speaker glides from the lecture room to "the mystical moist night-air." Because our reader is a good judge of human behavior, he realizes that there are those who find satisfaction in the lecture hall and there are others who find satisfaction in nature itself. His response of sympathetic pleasure arises, partly at least, from his observing that the speaker is acting in harmony with his own nature. Our reader will not attribute a failure in discipline to the speaker, first, because the reader judges human actions sympathetically and, second, because he sees nothing in the poem to suggest that the speaker is obligated to sit through the lecture.

The conception of this idealized, qualified reader is useful in thinking about, and in teaching, responsible literary comprehension and response. Matters of literary response cannot, finally, be resolved by finding answers to such a question as, "How do you as an individual respond to this selection?"

In a discussion, that kind of question may help a class get started. But if the comprehension of a literary text is the objective, an acceptable answer to the question must be verifiable from the particularities of the text along with right judgments of human behavior. The comprehension and appreciation of a literary work is one thing; unverifiable response to it is quite another.

Teaching the main cause of literary effects

The teaching of literary comprehension may start with a discussion of why people at all times and in all places have always liked stories. There is no need to be high-minded about this. Lead the students to see that our interest in stories may be explained by our interest in gossip or in other observations and depictions of human actions, thoughts, and emotions.

To translate these ideas into specific materials for discussion, relate such an incident as this: At 3:00 A.M. the woman next door hears a car stopping in front of the house across the street. She runs to the window and sees her neighbor's twenty-year-old daughter wave good-bye to a bearded and long-haired young man. Our observer of the scene forms an opinion of disapproval, and from this opinion experiences an emotion of shock.

From such discussions, help the class identify the mechanisms by which one's observations of human actions produce effects upon him. The mechanism may be stated as a three-step process:

1. Someone observes a span of human behavior or action.
2. The observer forms an opinion about that action.
3. The observer responds emotionally to the result of
   (a) what he observes and (b) his opinion about what he observes.

Next, ask the class to read a short and simple literary selection and apply this three-step process to it. Explain that each student is to be the observer of the action depicted.

For example, in John Updike's story, "A & P," we observe, in part, a young man, nineteen, arriving at an imprudent, self-defeating decision brought about largely by the rashness of youth. From observing this, we form an opinion that may be called an understanding tolerance of such rashness. We respond with a feeling of regret that there are unfortunate consequences from such impulsive, yet forgivable behavior. As another example, the earlier comments on "Learn'd Astronomer" show that the pleasurable effects depend upon our approval of the speaker's action. As indicated, approval is an opinion.

The discussions may refer to all sorts of human actions, actual or imaginary: real but disguised gossip, incidents, recollections, and so on. The literary examples may be those with which the class is familiar: a popular movie, a soap opera, or the latest production of the school's drama group. As a result of the discussions, these points should be established: (1) literature achieves its effects by depicting a sequence of human actions, (2) a natural interest in people and their actions explain our interest and the universal interest in literature, and (3) observers of human actions form opinions about them which arouse emotional responses.

A note on "identify with"

In everyday talk about their responses to fiction and drama, our students and people in general say that they "identify with" this or that character. By "identification" they seem to mean such approval of the actions of a character that they imagine themselves to be like him. To imagine one's self as a character may be prerequisite to acting, but it is not a principle of literary response. The reason is that a defensible comprehension and response arises from our observations of the actions of imaginary people and from our opinions of their actions. Our approval or other opinions of a particular character needs to be distinguished from our imagining that we are him.

One of the values of literature is that we are able to judge examples of human behavior without our selfishness distorting our judgment. The worlds of fiction aren't the world we live in, and the characters of fiction aren't threats to our well-being. That is why we can feel unselfish and sympathetic toward fictional characters. The notion conveyed by "identify with" suggests that we impose ourselves upon the fictional world. Such an imposition implies a distortion of the literary experience. Therefore, when students say that they "identify with," it is a good idea to explore with them just what they mean by this sense of "identification."

The exploration may begin with such a selection as "Learn'd Astronomer." Discuss, for example, these questions: "Does our response depend upon our being like the speaker?" "Why or why not?" "Must we be or think we must be the same kind of person that the speaker is if we are to respond properly to the poem?" "Why or why not?" "Does a defensible response to the poem depend upon our judgments of human actions generally?" "Why or why not?"

A rational discussion will clarify the principle that our responses to fictional characters and actions are the same as our responses to people and actions in the everyday world. The following conclusion, therefore, seems justified: Typical notions about identifying with characters are misleading and are best debunked and avoided.

Literary arguments

Everyone knows that there are literary selections whose intentions are to influence attitudes and actions toward matters in the world outside the selection. In the fable about the hare and the tortoise, for example, the purpose is the reader's realization that persevering effort can outstrip natural ability. Our interest is not mainly in the race but in the moral. A later example is *The Jungle,* a novel by Upton Sinclair. Its intention is to arouse the reader's indignation toward the unsanitary and inhuman conditions at an earlier time in Chicago's stockyards.

Arguments in literary form and in expository prose share similar purposes or effects and the same kinds of parts. Not only are such literary arguments presented in fables and novels, they are presented also in poems and plays. The widely anthologized poem by W. H. Auden, "The Unknown Citizen," exemplifies an argument, the effect of which is the reader's disturbance at the conformity and standardization of contemporary life. As an example of argumentative drama, the morality play *Everyman* comes immediately to mind.

Arguments in literary form do their work in the same way that arguments in expository prose do. Whether in expository or literary form, an argument is either inductive, deductive or analogical. In a literary argument, the action presented corresponds to one of the three kinds. *The Jungle* exemplifies inductive argument: We are to generalize from its action. Deductive action may be illustrated by *Everyman.* The characters, Fellowship, Worldly Goods, and Death are dramatic embodiments of generalities. We are to particularize from these. *Aesop's Fables* depict analogical action, as do the parables of Jesus. Such analogies imply a point-by-point correspondence between action and argument. For example, from the hare, we are to analogize to the overly confident, and from the tortoise, to the slow but sure.

These three modes of argument reflect the observations we all make about the incidents of everyday living. It is, therefore, convenient to help students clarify the modes of argument by referring to such incidents. I note, for example, that the man across the street is the father of five children but can't keep a job because he drinks too much. Consequently, his family is having a hard time getting by. From observing this particular action, I learn or learn more vividly that sobriety has its values. Put another way, I generalize from this action or example. Unknowingly, my alcoholic neighbor provides me with an example of inductive argumentative action.

For an example of everyday deductive action, let us consider the well-known reports that associate cigarette smoking with the incidence of lung cancer. From reading such a report, I particularize from it in the sense that I learn that cigarette smoking may be harmful to me. Notice that I am not drawing a conclusion from an instance as I do when I observe the behavior of my alcoholic neighbor.

Analogical arguments are demonstrated in instances that teach through point-by-point correspondence. I am in a strange city and having a hard time getting to an address. A helpful native tells me that I should turn right at the block ahead, go three more blocks, and turn left at Patroon Place. Because there is a point-by-point correspondence between the directions and the route I must follow, the directions constitute analogical explanation or argument.

To help students identify the methods by which incidents in the world and in everyday experience teach, refer to such current news items as exposés, scandals, obituaries, riots, and so on. Ask what these are likely to teach and whether the method is inductive, deductive, or analogical. Ask students what they have learned from everyday living, particularly through what specific incidents, and through which of the three modes of argument.

Represented actions

There are other literary works that so depict or represent the human actions of thought, feeling, and overt activity that we respond mainly to these rather than to issues outside the selection. I call such works "represented actions," a term taken from *Fiction and the Shape of Belief* by Sheldon Sacks.

The distinction between a literary argument and a represented action is absolute because it is based on purpose or final cause. As an example of represented action, the "Learn'd Astronomer" arouses our interest in the action itself. Notice that it is not an argument urging its readers to ditch lectures on astronomy. The poem is at pains to show that the lecture is well-worth hearing: the lecturer is "learn'd," well prepared with "charts and diagrams," and he receives "much applause." But all that is not for this speaker, and so he leaves. The speaker's action is not itself for everyone to follow, although the poem implies that one should be true to his own nature. This implication is a kind of truth that gives value to the action represented. (A discussion of the values built into literary works appears in the discussion on "significance" in this chapter.)

The implication that one should be true to his own nature, however, is not the "message" of the poem anymore than the notion that one should ditch lessons in astronomy. Being true to one's self is a value built into the poem that determines the qualified reader's pleased response. That pleased response constitutes the final cause. The final cause is not the reader's acceptance of the doctrine that one should be true to his own nature.

Literature organized by represented actions ranges from the shabbiest sex and murder novels to the sublimities of *Hamlet* and *Lear*. Some other familiar examples include *Macbeth*, "Miniver Cheevy," and John Updike's "A & P."

Distinguishing actions and arguments

Because arguments and represented actions are different, they imply differences in skills of comprehension and in methods of study. Therefore, students should be taught to distinguish one from the other. The distinction is not always simple and obvious. That is why students argue about the classification of a particular work. But issues can be arguable and yet resolvable through rational principles.

To teach how to distinguish one from the other, begin by presenting a pair of short poems or a pair of stories, one of the pair an argument, the other a represented action. Each should be a clear and unambiguous example of its kind. I have already cited "The Unknown Citizen," and "Learn'd Astronomer." Another such pair could be "The Unknown Citizen" (argument), and "Elegy for Jane" by Theodore Roethke (represented action). A pair of short stories could be "A & P" by John Updike (represented action), and *Prelude* by Albert Halper (argument). Presently this latter pair will be discussed.

There is no magic formula or secret key by which to infer the distinction. One reason is that the most compelling and carefully wrought argument may appear within a represented action, and the most fascinating represented action may appear within an argument. Another reason is the large and uncertain number of literary devices through which a work becomes one or the other.

The classification of a work in this sense requires that the reader determine whether he is mainly to be persuaded of a doctrine or affected by an action. To provide some clarification, a brief discussion of the stories indicated follows. The discussion is intended to suggest more explicitly the kind of inquiry to be carried out.

"Prelude" by Albert Halper is widely read in secondary schools, and it offers a clear example of literary argument. What is most vividly and affectingly put before the reader is a social problem, specifically, anti-Semitism. In presenting its argument, "anti-Semitism implies disastrous consequences," the story describes an incident that occurs in the late 1930s involving a Jewish newsstand dealer, his son, and his daughter. A gang of anti-Semitic young poolroom hoodlums without provocation disrupts the newsstand and publicly assaults the persons and dignity of the family. The people on the street, afraid, watch silently. Newspapers that the gang had thrown from the stand lay scattered along the sidewalk, displaying headlines about Hitler's incursions into Austria.

The story does not allay our concern about the welfare of the family after the incident. Rather, the story ends when its thesis is most fully and vividly demonstrated. Put another way, the family serves as agents to depict an issue.

It would have been possible for the author to use the social issue for making particularly vivid such human traits of the family as their fortitude, their loyalty to each other, and their maintaining self-respect under demeaning conditions. In such an instance, the story would have been a represented action.

Such an action is the organizing principle of "A & P." The nineteen-year-old narrator becomes aroused and fascinated by three swim-suited adolescent girls who enter the super-market. Upon noticing the girls, the manager reprimands them for their dress or lack of dress. Offended by this repri-mand, the narrator suddenly resigns his much-needed job in a pointless gesture of chivalry out of a misguided self-righteousness. Whatever social or moral issue is built into the story is outweighed by its unique human action.

As mentioned, the purpose of holding discussions of these and similar pairs of poems and stories is the students' ability to distinguish arguments and actions. To do this, they must inquire into just what it is that determines the principle by which a work is organized. In "Prelude," for example, the end comes when the rhetorical point is established and not when the human consequences of the situation is resolved. In "A & P," however, the story ends with the probable or necessary consequences of the narrator's behavior.

But mere endings don't always explain. The student must learn to identify whatever the devices may be by which a work becomes an action or an argument. We must guard against accepting such a statement as this: "X is a represented action because it mainly presents a human action." For that kind of statement to be acceptable, it must be followed by an explanation of just what sequential action is presented and just how a qualified reader is to respond to it. In conduct-ing the discussion, encourage the students to work from effects to the causes that are incorporated into the work and to continue this until there is a convincing interpretation, com-pletely justified by the particularities of the text along with everyday knowledge about human behavior.

"Author's role"

Poetry and fiction necessarily present their arguments and actions through speakers and narrators. It is conventional to refer to "speakers" of poems and to "narrators" of stories and novels. When the speaker or narrator is not a character in the work, students often refer to the speaker as the poet and the narrator as the author. This practice requires further inquiry.

Whether the speaker of "Learn'd Astronomer" is Whitman is not a matter of comprehension as it is defined here. Rather, the issue is one of historical or literary biography. The literary question concerns the suitability of the speaker, whoever he may be, to the effects of the poem.

On the surface, certain examples seem to argue against this principle: Although Matthew Arnold's "Rugby Chapel" is not about to take the high school by storm, the example it provides is instructive. The speaker is obviously Arnold himself. But this kind of instance does not affect the principle at issue. For "Rugby Chapel" to do its work, it has to represent Arnold as an able, sensitive, and respectful son. This example shows that if we are to explain relationships between artistic effects and their causes, we must explain, among other matters, the appropriateness of speakers and narrators to the wholes of which they are parts. Biographical considerations in a historical sense are the concerns of other, but equally valid, methods of literary study.

Narrators in plays

Although poetry and fiction must depict through speakers and narrators, drama represents its arguments and actions through enactment on the stage. In such plays as *Our Town* and *The Glass Menagerie*, however, there are personages who perform narrations. Our students must not be allowed to fall into the trap (for very long) of being confused between narration on the stage and narration of fiction and poetry. However unconventional, narrations (and soliloquies) in drama are as much staged incidents as the balcony scene of *Romeo and Juliet* is.

To help students clarify the distinction, ask them to discuss such questions as these: "How are poems and stories made available to us?" "How is a play made available to us?" "In *Our Town* (or *The Glass Menagerie*) does the narrator do the same work (or perform the same function) as the speaker in

'Learn'd Astronomer' or the narrator in 'A & P?' Why or why not?"

The result of such discussion should help the class arrive at these conclusions: (1) Speakers and narrators make poems and fiction available to their readers. (2) Acting on the stage makes plays available to their audiences. (3) Narrations and soliloquies in plays are incidents and not themselves means of making the entire play available to the audience.

The literal sense of what is going on in a work

Language, which is the material that poems and fiction are made of, can depict only the human actions of thought, emotion, and overt activity. To this contention, one may say that language can depict animals, mountains, and a wrecked automobile. Such depictions, however, are necessarily forms of thought or human conceptions of such nonhuman objects.

Overt action and thought may be directly depicted, but feelings must be inferred from noting thought and action. We infer a state of grief, for example, from noting that the person cries or that he expresses thoughts that reveal his emotions.

All human actions, thoughts, and feelings occur in time-bound or temporal order. An argument in prose, for instance, presents a chronologically ordered set of subarguments or details. The argument of "Prelude" presents chronologically ordered incidents from which we generalize, demonstrating thereby inductive action. A work organized by a represented action affects us by its action being sequential and coherent.

In teaching to comprehend, therefore, it is indispensable that students be able to identify the action completely and accurately. Too often, students take a part of the action for all of it. The action of "Learn'd Astronomer" for example, is not merely the speaker's sitting in the lecture hall, becoming bored, leaving, and then enjoying the "mystical, moist night-air." Rather, the complete action to which we respond includes the speaker's recollection of the incident he describes. Put differently, in "Learn'd Astronomer" we respond to a particular speaker's recollection of an incident, not merely to the incident he recollects. A recollection is as much a literary action as a cops-and-robbers chase is.

Similarly, in *The Glass Menagerie* the action is not merely the sequence of incidents that occurs in the Wingfield's apartment. The complete action consists of Tom Wingfield's recollections of, and observations on, that sequence of incidents. As Tom says, he is presenting a "memory play."

As other examples, in "Stopping by Woods on a Snowy Evening," the action is not merely the speaker's sitting in his sleigh, observing the falling snow, and then moving on. Rather, the complete action consists of the speaker's depiction of, and comments on, that incident. The represented action of "John Anderson, My Jo" by Robert Burns is not merely the long and happy marriage. The full action includes the wife's recollection of all this. The action in "A & P" is not merely what happens, but the narrator's recollections of, and comments on, what had happened.

In different words, the action to which we respond in "Learn'd Astronomer," *The Glass Menagerie*, "John Anderson," and "A & P" consists of time-bound recollections of certain experiences. The action to which we respond in "Stopping by Woods . . . ," however, is not a recollection but the depiction of an action as the speaker participates in it.

In the works just considered, there is a correspondence between the action and the text presented to the reader. The "Learn'd Astronomer," for instance, presents directly and straightforwardly the sequence of recollections that constitutes the action to which we respond.

In some other works, however, there is a disjunction between the action and the text presented to the reader. Consider, for example, this poem by William Carlos Williams:

> This Is Just to Say
> I have eaten
> the plums
> that were in
> the icebox
>
> and which
> you were probably

saving
for breakfast

Forgive me
they were delicious
so sweet
and so cold[3]

After reading this poem, we arrive, intuitively, at the idea that it is organized by a represented action. Looking more closely, we observe that what appears on the page is a note to someone. A note to someone is itself a thing rather than an action. In a represented action, we are affected by the action rather than by things themselves. Therefore, if we are to explain why we sense that the poem is an action, we must try to infer just what that temporal action is. By reading this note or poem, we easily and reasonably infer the following as the time-bound action: The writer of the note had a yen for the plums and ate them. Fearing the addressee's annoyance at this, the writer wrote the note to explain and assuage. Along with this action, we infer that it's a summer's night ("plums") before the days of refrigerators ("icebox"), and that the writer and the addressee of the note won't see each other until the next morning.

Although the represented action and the inferences related to it constitute the main interest, we analogize to all kinds of similar situations in which the indulgence of natural, innocent desires gives us pleasure but gets in the way of prudent practicality. The poem votes for pleasure. Of this temporal action, the poem presents only the note. From this, the reader infers the rest. To say that the poem is what literally appears on the page is to suggest the reading of the words, but the missing of the action.

"This Is Just to Say," then, is a represented action depicted by a note. There are other actions depicted by a series of notes or letters. This is a widely used literary device. For example, Ring Lardner's story, "Some Like Them Cold," consists of a series of letters from which we infer the following action: A young man and a young woman meet in a Chicago railroad station. The man, an opportunistic writer of popular songs, is about to board the train for New York City, where he hopes to make his fortune. The two correspond. In her letters to him, she represents herself as possessing wifely and domestic traits and qualities. Despite this, however, the man finally marries a woman who is cold, selfish, demanding, and self-indulgent.

Some plays that are organized by a represented action exhibit other kinds of disjunction between action and what is presented directly to the audience. In *King Lear* the action doesn't begin until Lear asks his daughters about their love for him, for that is the point at which his troubles start. Arthur Miller's play, *The Price*, presents on the stage only the end of its temporal action, which begins years before when the protagonist, Victor Franz, abandoned his plan to become a scientist and, instead, joined the police force.

To review and clarify: Language can depict only the human actions of thought, emotion, and overt activity. These occur in temporal order. When we are to be affected by a represented action, the literary selection must either depict that action directly or it must be so constructed that we may infer the action. Thoughts, recollections, and emotions, in this view, are as much actions as fist fights. In some selections, there is complete correspondence between the text of the work or the incidents on the stage and the actions that these depict. Other selections, however, depict directly only some or even none of their actions. In such instances, we must infer the action from whatever constitutes the text of the poem, play, or fiction.

The foregoing discussion suggests the need to teach students to identify the entire action, however particular works may represent them. Begin with selections in which action and text correspond. Ask them to identify the action. Their almost inevitable failures at first to give acceptable answers are opportunities to help them correct their misapprehensions and to help them identify the whole. Typically, the misapprehensions are failures to note that the work of speakers and narrators is part and parcel of the action.

Later, discuss in similar fashion selections in which there are disjunctions between action on the one hand and text or scenario on the other. Some examples have already been given. The materials for discussion may include letters written to such newspaper advisors as Ann Landers and Abigail Van Buren. Such letters of inquiry often make it easy to infer amusing, pitiful, or outlandish represented actions.

Discuss popular fare also: movies, soap operas, television plays, and the like. The film *They Shoot Horses, Don't They?* exemplifies a striking disjunction between action and scenario. The action begins with an aspiring actress in straitened circumstances who becomes so financially desperate that she enters a dance marathon in an attempt to survive. The marathon brings still more suffering to her as she undergoes humiliation and physical torment. When she learns that even if she were to win the marathon she wouldn't get the prize money because the promoter is unscrupulous, she and her partner quit. Unable now to go on living, she attempts suicide but is unable to pull the trigger. Her partner understands, and kills her at her request. The scenario of the film, however, presents mainly the marathon itself and its accompanying miseries. From this and a series of brief flashbacks and flashforwards, the spectator infers the entire action.

Significance in represented actions

We have been considering represented actions as causes of emotional effects. The effects of such actions, however, are not emotional only. When we observe human behavior, actual or imaginary, we unavoidably bring to it ethical values. These values are ethical in the sense that we judge the actions that we observe; judging implies notions of good and bad, right and wrong, important and unimportant, and so on. Because represented actions imply values, the study of literature offers ethical contributions to school learning. To refer to this ethical aspect of literature, I use the term "significance."

The teaching of significance in literature is obviously of first importance. Let us consider, then, (1) the logical basis of such teaching and (2) an explanation and illustration of its practice.

We begin with the proposition that an art requires a perfection or at least an adequacy of the sense that it addresses. Music, for example, is not addressed to the deaf, nor are painting and sculpture addressed to the blind. Literature presents human actions, and these imply moral and ethical judgments. Therefore, literature addresses the moral sense and assumes a perfection of it. As explained, the qualified reader is a hypothetical ideal possessing a perfected moral sense. By "moral," I mean, roughly, the qualified reader's approval or disapproval of an action.

To explain further, in the section above, "Teaching the main cause of literary effects," I show that in literature, as in life, we observe an action, form an opinion or judgment about it, and then respond emotionally. Our judgments fall somewhere on a scale from disapproval to approval, contempt to admiration, bad to good, and so on. Such judgments imply values that we hold and values that are built into the work.

Moreover, in literature we observe actions that are imaginary, a condition that offers opportunity to judge without our selfishness interfering with our judgment. Therefore, we can judge generously, sympathetically, and therefore properly. The proper judgment of human behavior is a problem that everyone faces all his life. This ability to judge may be improved through the kind of study that we are now discussing.

The teaching implied may be clarified by inquiring into what we do when we demonstrate understanding of the significance of literature. Turning again to the "Learn'd Astronomer," we approve of the speaker's leaving the lecture hall because he is acting in accordance with his own nature. That is the value incorporated into the poem and the value that we hold as well. In "This Is Just to Say," the value is perhaps less important: enjoying innocent pleasures that get in the way of prudent practicality. "A & P" incorporates the value of prudence in difficult situations. Our feeling of regret stems from the narrator's failure, however understandable, to exercise good judgment in what to him is a difficult situation.

The foregoing illustrations suggest that inquiry into literary significance requires that we identify the values incorporated into the work and compare these with our own. These illustrations suggest, further, that in works of at least respectable literary quality, our values and those in the selection are likely to correspond, although they need not. With selections of ordinary or inferior quality, however, the values in the work are not likely to arouse our serious concern.

Consider, for example, the kind of love or success story that appears in a *True Story* type of magazine. Typically, ordinary, predictable characters get themselves mates or promotions by overcoming this or that hindrance to their goals. Usually, the values in those works are simply those of getting what you want. Such fiction aims at entertainment pure and simple, and no one will confuse "Romance on Fifth Avenue" with *The Old Man and the Sea*.

The foregoing discussion implies specific procedures for teaching. By identifying the objectives, we may infer the procedures. There are four interrelated skills, and, therefore, four objectives:

1. To identify the chronological action to which we are to respond.
2. To identify the emotional effect produced by that action.
3. To identify the values built into the work and our own that affect our opinion of the action.
4. To explain the relationships among the action, the values and opinions, and the emotional response.

By applying the skills to "This Is Just to Say," we have already identified the action; the effect is a sympathetic pleasure at the speaker's indulging in an innocent, natural delight; and the value in the work, as mentioned, is that of enjoying innocent pleasures that get in the way of prudent practicality. We approve of the action because we hold the same value that the speaker does, which leads to the effect of sympathetic pleasure.

In actual teaching, begin with whatever short, reputable selections that may be at hand. For each, translate the four objectives into questions and discuss with the class the answers given. Extend the inquiry by reading to them a story that appears in such publications as *True Story*. Ask them to identify the values built into these stories and to compare these values with those of a qualified reader and with those incorporated into works of more respectable quality. Through such discussions, we may teach the distinction between good and bad literature through rational principles.

Such discussions should not degenerate into hunts for morals. Here, I use "morals" to refer to preaching. Put differently, our students should not confuse values with morals in this latter sense. As mentioned, values are ideas of what is important or unimportant, and so forth. It is hardly the intention of "Learn'd Astronomer" to preach the message, "We should act in accordance with our natures." Everyone knows that in an imperfect world, such behavior is not feasible. Further, the function of values, ideas, and beliefs in represented actions is to enhance the value and interest of the action. For arguments in literary form, the reverse is true: in such works, the action functions to enhance the ideas, beliefs, and doctrines.

This study of significance offers certain intellectual and emotional conditions that contribute to a student's inquiry into ethical principles and actions. Such contributions, however, should not be confused with the illusion that literature, however high its moral value, can itself directly inculcate the habit of ethical behavior.

Degrees of seriousness

The discussion just concluded suggests that we take the more valuable to be more serious than we do the less valuable. I am using "serious" to refer to matters of such concern to us that they affect us with considerable intensity of emotion. In this sense, the "Learn'd Astronomer" is more serious than "This Is Just to Say." *Macbeth* is more serious than *The Importance of Being Earnest*. Willa Cather's "Paul's Case" is more serious than "The Secret Life of Walter Mitty." The serious element in a represented action, however, does not itself determine the artistic merit of the whole.

So that student may increase their awareness of literary responses, they should be taught to identify effects as serious and less serious and to explain how these effects are caused. Start by asking what it is in everyday life that we take to be more and less serious. Specifically, ask them to consider a minor cut on one's finger and the loss of an arm. From such a discussion, develop the idea that we take the permanent and the long-lasting to be more serious than the temporary. Ask what kinds of people we take more and less seriously. Arrive at the idea that we tend to take seriously those who in some moral, historical, or intellectual sense we believe to exceed the ordinary, and that we take the ordinary less seriously. Ask what kinds of questions or issues we consider to be more serious and less serious. From such a discussion, develop the conception that the serious issues are those concerning the relationships between the people and their government, their God, their work, and so on, while the matter of who should be elected dog catcher is less serious.

Consider, also, what it is that strikes people more seriously than the content of the matter would suggest. Ask which affects our emotions more powerfully, the death of an ordinary person who was a friend or neighbor or the death by earthquake of 10,000 natives of Iran. Develop the idea that we take more seriously the close-at-hand and what immediately affects us than matters that are remote and that have no immediate influence upon our welfare.

Such a discussion may be extended to the action in literature. Ask them to identify the degree of seriousness in the action incorporated into the literary work at hand and to explain the reason why the work is serious, not serious, or somewhere in between. Further, ask them to compare the degrees of seriousness of works recently read. Referring to the kinds of paired selections cited in the first paragraph of this section, ask them to explain the reasons for the degrees of seriousness in each pair.

Avoiding misguided symbol hunts

As a result of dubious literary training, some readers have acquired the mistaken notion that imaginative literature, unlike expository prose, doesn't mean what it says. In this view the reader imposes upon a literary work meanings that the text cannot justify.

As an example, the speaker in "Stopping by the Woods. . ." has at times been said to be a symbol of death, or of something other than what the text represents him as being: a thoughtful and responsible person who is sensitive to beauty. The text cannot sustain other than literal interpretations because what it literally says constitutes a complete poem and all of its words are fully used up in conveying its action. Further, the text is not illuminated by imposing upon its words, meanings that are external to what the poem is explicitly stating. To assume that readers are free to impose on texts any meanings they wish is to assume that the study of literature is not a rational inquiry, but rather an exercise in free association.

Some texts, however, clearly imply symbolic interpretation. "Ex-Basketball Player" by John Updike is one example. The action of the poem consists of an intelligent narrator's description of Flick Webb, who was an outstanding high-school basketball star but now, locked into a dead-end job, is a mere pumper of gas and changer of tires. The contrast between his earlier local fame and his hopeless present explains his depressed state of mind. Notice the first stanza of the poem that follows:

Ex-Basketball Player

Pearl Avenue runs past the high school lot,
Bends with the trolley tracks, and stops, cut off
Before it has a chance to go two blocks,
At Colonel McComsky Plaza. Berth's Garage
Is on the corner facing west, and there,
Most days, you'll find Flick Webb, who helps Berth out.

Flick stands tall among the idiot pumps—
Five on a side, the old bubble-head style,
Their rubber elbows hanging loose and low.
One's nostrils are two S's, and his eyes
An E and O. And one is squat, without
A head at all—more of a football type.

Once, Flick played for the high school team, the Wizards.

He was good: in fact, the best. In '46,
He bucketed three hundred ninety points,
A county record still. The ball loved Flick.
I saw him rack up thirty-eight or forty
In one home game. His hands were like wild birds.

He never learned a trade; he just sells gas,
Checks oil, and changes flats. Once in a while,
As a gag, he dribbles an inner tube,
But most of us remember anyway.
His hands are fine and nervous on the lug wrench.
It makes no difference to the lug wrench, though.

Off work, he hangs around Mae's Luncheonette.
Grease-grey and kind of coiled, he plays pinball,
Sips lemon cokes, and smokes those thin cigars;
Flick seldom speaks to Mae, just sits and nods
Beyond her face towards bright applauding tiers
of Necco Wafers, Nibs, and Juju Beads.[4]

We assume that writers, particularly poets, make purposeful, deliberate choice of their words, images, and ideas, and so on. Therefore, such choices as these must be accounted for: "Pearl Avenue," the cutting off of that avenue, "Berth," and "facing west." The remainder of the poem justifies these inferences: the cutting off of Pearl Avenue parallels the cutting off of Flick's career on the basketball court; "Berth" is suggestive of "berth" in the sense of one's place or station in life: Berth's Garage, then, suggests Flick's particular place in society; and "facing west," a conventional symbol of the end, is analogous to Flick's dead-end situation. Further evidence in support of these interpretations may be found in these facts: The complete story of Flick Webb is told after this opening stanza, and the details incorporated into the first stanza and that stanza as a whole have no other function than to prepare the reader for the narrator's depiction of the unfortunate ex-basketball player.

In teaching and reading literature, then, begin with the assumption that the work means what it says. Attribute symbolic or metaphoric interpretations only after it is clear that the words and ideas must be there for reasons other than

154 FUNDAMENTALS FOR TEACHING LITERATURE

literal statement. Finally, infer the symbolic or metaphorical meanings by showing that such non-literal meanings contribute to the whole and to its effects.

Pitfalls

In its degradations, the teaching of literature is a means to improved composition, to the study of grammar, to the direct inculcation of morals, or to some ends other than those uniquely suited to literary selections. The teaching of literary response is distorted when the responses are conceived as matters of identifying with characters or as whatever reactions to literature students say they have without reference to the text. A related perversion is caused by a failure to distinguish the work as an argument or as a represented action. Poetry and fiction are mistaught when the function of narration is disregarded and the action is said to be merely that which is narrated.

Still another example of misteaching, particularly of represented actions, occurs when what appears on the page or on the stage is *always* assumed to constitute the action to which we respond. A further misguided practice is to impose upon literary texts symbols or metaphors that the text cannot justify. Finally, inquiry into values and significance in literature is misguided when the literary selection is taken to be a text for moral preaching rather than an object for discovering its values and its aesthetic pleasures.

Summary

1. The values and the universal interest in literature together with its variety and abundance raises the problem of matching students with books. Certain kinds of classroom discussions as well as libraries and booklists help resolve that problem.

2. Analysis aids appreciation. If analysis kills it, then something may be wrong with the kind of analysis but not with the principle that increased understanding fosters appreciation.

3. To study literature is to work with primary sources. Proper literary study implies the use of critical principles at whatever level of performance is suitable for the student.

4. The intended reader of good literature is intelligent, prudent, and humane. He may be called a "qualified reader," a conception that is useful in clarifying problems or literary comprehension and response.

5. The main cause of literary effects is a chronologically-ordered human action involving thought, emotion, and overt activity. An understanding of that resolves many problems of comprehension.

6. The popular notion that readers and audiences "identify with" certain characters is misconceived and, therefore, conveys a misunderstanding of literary inquiry.

7. A particular work of literature is organized either by an argument or by a represented action. Each of these organizing principles implies consequences for literary comprehension and response.

8. If there is a narrator in a play, he has a different function from the narrator of a work of fiction and the speaker of a poem.

9. The reader's failure to identify the entire action that the work brings to him explains a common misreading of literature.

10. Values are necessarily built into poems, plays, and fiction; these values imply coherent procedures by which to discover the social and moral significance of particular works.

11. A work of literature means what it says unless there is evidence for implying symbolic or metaphoric interpretation.

Exercises

Exercise 1

Search in educational literature for suggestions on how to stimulate secondary school students to acquire the habit of reading for fun. List the suggestions that seem to you to be particularly promising. Give reasons for your choices.

Exercise 2

Select any poem, play, or story organized by a represented action that you think you'd like to teach a class of secondary school students. Read it in order to anticipate problems the class is likely to have. The problems may include vocabulary, topical and other allusions, and the literal sense of what is going on in the work. How would you help the students with the difficulties?

Exercise 3

Typically, a teacher asks, "What is this story about?" and the student then restates the story as it is presented on the page. Assume that the comprehension of short stories is the goal. Comment on this familiar problem.

Exercise 4

The selection that follows may be viewed as a represented action. Further, the selection is an example of a work in which action and its presentation or depiction do not completely correspond.

> Dear Ann Landers: A widow of 67, confined to my bed, I've found a man in his 20's who truly loves me. Monty, who gave up a steady job in a gas station to move in and care for me, is a dream, joking with me, feeding me cocoa and making me take my medicine. My jealous children insist he's a fortune hunter, and their nagging has made me sicker. Monty tried to dissuade me from naming him my sole heir, but I've done it just to show them. Their callousness has made me so weak and hazy, I can barely finish this letter. Please tell me what to do about my ungrateful children.*

(a) Identify the action. (b) State relationships between the action and its representation. (c) Formulate a set of ideal questions and ideal replies to each question that are intended to help students distinguish the action from its depiction on the page.

*Copyright © 1970 by the NYM Corp. Reprinted with the permission of NEW YORK Magazine. Written by Lawrence Eisenberg for NEW YORK Magazine Competition Number fifty-two. Mary Ann Madden is the author of the Competition.

Exercise 5

Select a poem, story, play, or novel that you think ought to be taught in a secondary school and state the grade or range of grades at which you think it ought to be taught. Describe how you would use that selection for the teaching of literary significance. Explain your procedures in terms of Level 3 objectives, learning activities, the organization of learning activities, and evaluation. In your description of learning activities, be specific in formulating the questions you would ask and the ideal answers you would expect.

Notes

1. John Dewey, "My Pedagogic Creed" (1897), in Daniel J. Boorstin, ed., *An American Primer* (Mentor Books; New York: New American Library, 1966), p. 639.

2. Most of the literary principles discussed in this chapter have been taken from such writings as those listed in Chapter 2, note 3, particularly *Tragedy and the Theory of Drama* by Elder Olson.

3. From William Carlos Williams, *Collected Earlier Poems* (New York: New Directions, 1938).

4. From John Updike, *The Carpentered Hen and Other Tame Creatures* (New York: Harper & Row, 1957); originally published in *The New Yorker.*

CHAPTER 7

THE COMPREHENSION OF LYRIC POETRY

The chapter explains and illustrates how the principles of literary comprehension may be used in the teaching of lyric poetry. Such comprehension implies the use of part-whole skills.

The systematic study of literary comprehension may begin with lyric poetry; the brevity of the form makes it convenient as a starting point.

Teaching literal-sense comprehension

To illustrate the "literal-sense" objective described in Chapter 6, I use a familiar poem by Robert Herrick, which I have found appealing to students of varying abilities, grade levels, and social classes. Although this poem has long been familiar and widely anthologized, it is typically misunderstood even in its "literal sense." Our use of this poem, then, illustrates the need to look at the entire human action that the poem brings to the reader.

> To the Virgins, to Make Much of Time
>
> Gather ye rose-buds while ye may,
>> Old Time is still a-flying,
> And this same flower that smiles today,
>> Tomorrow will be dying.
>
> The glorious lamp of heaven, the Sun,
>> The higher he's a-getting,

The sooner will his race be run,
And nearer he's to setting.

That age is best which is the first,
When youth and blood are warmer;
But being spent, the worse, the worst
Times still succeed the former.

Then be not coy, but use your time,
And while ye may, go marry;
For having lost but once your prime,
You may forever tarry.

A first step is to introduce students to the poem. That means relating what the poem says to their experience. There is an uncertain number of ways to do it. One is to ask them whether they have heard of unmarried young women being urged to get married. Next, tell them that we are going to consider how this urging is done in a good poem.

A second step is anticipating difficulties they are likely to have with vocabulary. Only a simple, straightforward explanation is needed. Write on the board the difficult words and their glosses. For this poem, the glosses are likely to be these:

virgins	unmarried young women
still	always
tarry	wait

Explain that the poet lived in the seventeenth century ("the 1600s"), and that the meanings of some English words have changed from the way he used them.

A third step is the oral reading of the poem. The students have a printed copy that they can follow silently. Before reading, however, ask them to answer a broad question pertinent to the poem. For example, "What is the action that the poem presents to the reader?" The poem is then read aloud. The oral reading should convey clearly the sense of the poem. Students should not be asked to read to the class orally unless they have already studied the poem and practiced reading it. No one should be expected to listen to an inept oral reading.

With the oral reading completed, ask for replies to the question posed earlier. During the discussion, insist upon replies that are justified by reference to the poem. It is impossible to predict just what miscomprehensions will be revealed by a given discussion. The guide for conducting the discussion is the desired achievement—the student's skill in getting the literal sense. Ideally, the discussion should clear away problems that may be revealed, and thus clarify the poem's action.

It is likely that the responses will be the conventional ones, which may be expressed somewhat as follows: The "poet" is telling some young women to get married while they can, and by implication he is urging upon readers the moral to make hay while the sun shines.

The particularities of the text, however, will not sustain this conventional interpretation. In the first place, the speaker is hardly the poet, but some other person who is preachy yet skilled in argumentation and in the metaphorical use of language. In the second place, the speaker is not addressing the reader but the young women who seem to him to need the advice. In the third place, the advice itself is a platitude or commonplace that the qualified reader has no need of. The action presented, therefore, is an incident in which an articulate, poetic but preachy speaker, noting a bevy of un-married young women, takes it upon himself to provide advice in the form of a carefully constructed argument in support of a commonplace. The effect upon the reader, then, is not his being informed or persuaded, but rather his being lightheartedly amused by the admonition and pleased by the exquisite poetic expression, the sound effects, and the inge-nuity of the argument.

The conventional interpretation of the poem exemplifies the fault of mistaking an aspect for the entire action. When such a mistake occurs, the student should be asked to return to the text and to reconstruct by means of appropriate ques-tions just what it is that the poem is depicting. Some exam-ples of useful questions:

What kind of person is the speaker?
What is the situation to which the speaker is reacting?
Who is the speaker addressing?
What, mainly, is the speaker's response to the situation?

From looking at the entire incident, how is the reader expected to respond?

Do not "hold them responsible" for the poem by threatening them with a test or examination on it. My experience suggests that by holding enjoyable discussions on enjoyable poems, students become gradually but surely more adept at apprehending the literal sense, more responsible in their comments during discussion, and increasingly interested in poetry.

The kind of procedure just outlined may profitably constitute the greater part of literary study, especially at its beginning. When the class seems to have progressed appreciably toward the desired proficiency, then evaluate more formally. Present the students with a poem within their experience but one that presumably they haven't seen before, and ask them to state the literal sense of what is going on in it. The results will reveal strengths and weaknesses of the instruction.

Teaching part-whole comprehension

To explain the teaching of part-whole comprehension, I shall refer mainly to "Dust of Snow." In discussing it, I shall briefly identify effects, whole, nonverbal and verbal parts, and the functioning of these parts.

Dust of Snow

The way a crow
Shook down on me
The dust of snow
From a hemlock tree

Has given my heart
A change of mood
And saved some part
Of a day I had rued.

Robert Frost[1]

By now, it is clear that a represented action differs from an editorial. The editorial presents an argument and the lyric presents, essentially, a human action for the sake of arousing emotions of pleasure and pain, and for conveying certain values. Further, the language of lyrics is typically a source of pleasure. But pleasure from the use of words is accessible to all forms of writing.

For lyrics as represented actions, then, the part-whole skills differ from those for arguments in prose, and for two reasons: First, the effects of such lyrics are emotional rather than persuasive in the usual rhetorical sense; second, these lyrics present mainly a human action rather than an argument. The following discussion of "Dust of Snow," explains more fully what the parts and skills mean.

The intended effects may be described as two mutually supporting kinds of pleasure. One kind is sympathetic and is aroused by the action depicted. The other pleasure is that aroused by admiring a discourse in which diction, rhythm, and rhyme are suited to the experience and convey pleasing patterns of sound. The human action is that of a sensitive person who recollects that his mood had changed from dejection to some happier state when a crow shook snow down on him. That is the experience that elicits the effects.

In "Dust of Snow," we infer from what the speaker says that he is the kind of person who is sensitive to nature and language; his state of mind, he suggests to us, was sad ("day I had rued"), but becomes happier upon experiencing the dust of snow ("Has given my heart/A change of mood"). Although the experience is not a momentous one, it is to be taken seriously.

The action is brought before the reader in a particular way, or through a particular set of non-verbal parts. To convey the experience and to arouse the effects, a particular selection of details must be presented. In good poetry, the details put before the reader are only those needed for the poem to do its job. In "Dust of Snow," these are essentially a recollection of a crow shaking down snow from a hemlock tree onto the speaker, and the speaker's responses to this. The hemlock, an evergreen, collects snow on its branches and needles. Its branches are usually flexible; it is likely, therefore, that when a crow lights on a snow-covered hemlock, some snow will be shaken down.

The character of the speaker has already been noted. Because the poem requires sensitivity to mood, nature, and language, the selection of this kind of speaker is required. He relates the occurrence after it has happened. Such a point of view is suitable because it is improbable that he would express his "change of mood" so well unless he had time to reflect. It is fitting, too, that the speaker himself relates the experience. An action is more convincing when it is related by the one who experienced it. This holds particularly for experiences that are uniquely personal, as this one is.

Emphasis means the extent to which the details or sections are rendered more or less prominent or striking. One obvious means is time or space. Usually, the more one talks or writes about something, the greater the emphasis. Prominence or emphasis may be conveyed through still other means. One is vividness. Another is surprise.

The term "order" means the sequence in which the details are presented. In discussing "Dust of Snow," it is convenient to treat order and emphasis together.

The two stanzas correspond to the two main divisions of the poem. In the first, the speaker describes the snow being shaken down on him. In the second, he describes two consequences brought on by that occurrence: his mood had been changed and some part of his day had been saved. Thus, situation and response to it explain the order, and our pleasure that things came out well for someone we like.

A division into two stanzas partly explains the emphasis. Emphasis in each is about the same, but for different reasons. The first stanza produces a striking effect because of the scene that it calls to the imagination. The second stanza, although less striking, is more emotionally affecting because it describes a transition from a state of sadness to one of happiness. Again this helps explain the pleasurable effects.

How to talk about the language of a poem

Throughout, the discussion of nonverbal parts is always related to their functions. Because language is also a part, the purpose of discussing it is to clarify its function within the whole. There is little point in treating metaphor, rhyme, and metrics as discrete and isolated phenomena. In the discussion that follows, language is treated as a functioning part.

Typically, lyric poems are characterized by brevity of depiction and by precision, compactness, and economy of expression. They are characterized, further, by a distinctive diction and such embellishments as rhythm, rhyme, alliteration, and the like. These and similar devices of language serve also as one means for unifying a poem. Language in poetry, therefore, functions to form unified discourse characterized by economy of means and verbal ornament; it is to such matters that this part of the inquiry is aimed.

"Dust of Snow" depicts the experience briefly, simply, appropriately, and with pleasing sounds and verbal ornament, all within a discourse both unified and symmetrical. Its language helps it do these things. The experience is a brief one: The poem has only thirty-four words, all of them plain and simple. Thirty-two are one syllable. The other two are "hemlock" and "given." The metaphor "dust" briefly suggests the appearance and texture of the snow.

Brevity of experience and simplicity of depiction are conveyed not only through words but also through syntax. The poem, syntactically, is a single sentence. The first stanza is the subject and consists of a single nominal. Grammatically, one may substitute the word "it" for the first stanza. The last stanza is a compound predicate. This grammatical relationship conveys the main features of the action. First, the external scene and occurrence are conveyed by the subject and, second, the two consequences are presented in the predicate with each of the two finite verbals: "Has given" and "saved."

Not only is simplicity suggested by short, simple words and simple syntax, but also by short lines. Shortness of line in coordination with simple words and syntax convey an overall effect of succinctness. This brevity and simplicity are appropriate for at least two reasons. First, the simplicity of language is suited to the elemental experience. Second, this sense of the fitness of things suggests the speaker's sensitivity to language.

Another example of language suited to purpose appears in

the poem's last line. It consists of six syllables, while the other lines consist of four or five. All lines fit the overall metrical pattern. In the last, however, the greater number of syllables has the effect of slowing down the utterance and of thereby lending a sense of finality. That assertion may be tested by oral reading.

Unity of effect is caused by unity of discourse. Not only is the unity of this poem achieved largely through a coherent relationship between external situation and its consequences, but also through patterned repetition of sound. One pattern is the rhyme scheme: a b a b   c d c d. Another is the meter, iambic dimeter, which is sustained throughout. Apart from their uses as means of unity, the patterned rhyme and meter themselves give pleasure.

The foregoing discussion illustrates how language is used to make a poem an ordered, unified discourse characterized partly by economy of means and pleasing words suited to what is expressed. The discussion has suggested how learners may be taught to inquire into the language of poems. Typical works may be approached with these four questions:

What devices of language (e.g., diction, syntax, meter, figures of speech, sounds) depict the experience or argument?

What devices of language help the poem achieve unity?

What devices of language help the poem convey the experience or argument briefly and compactly?

Through what devices does the language itself convey particular pleasures?

Other questions, also, may be framed as means for increased understanding of the function of language. This inquiry is not based on preconceived ideas of what characteristics of language are proper to poetry. Instead, the inquiry is aimed at discovering how language in a particular poem functions to create its peculiar effects and unique characteristics. When a teacher and class identify these effects and characteristics, the questions become almost self-evident: If, for example, a characteristic of a poem is brevity and compact-

PART-WHOLE SKILLS FOR COMPREHENDING POEMS ORGANIZED BY REPRESENTED ACTIONS

1. *Purpose:* (a) Describe the intended emotional effect on a continuum of serious–not serious. (b) Justify response to (a) by explicit reference to the text.

2. *Form:* Describe the action that the poem presents. Formulate that description in such fashion that your reader or listener can see the time-bound action, whether mainly mental, emotional, or overt. State relationships between the effect upon the reader and the experience that the poem depicts.

3. *Nonverbal parts:* For each part listed below (a) identify the part, (b) justify the response to (a) by explicit reference to the text, and (c) state how the part functions toward producing the effect. As a result of inquiry into the parts labeled 3.1 to 6.6, the reader should be able to explain what is presented (3.4), in what order (3.5), to what extent (3.6), and in what light (3.1 and 3.2).

   3.1. The personal qualities of the speaker.

   3.2. The attitudes he conveys toward the experience he depicts, his audience, and himself. (Usually only one of these attitudes is dominant. Account only for the single dominant attitude.)

   3.3. The relations between the time of narration or representation and the time at which an action occurs.

   3.4. The set of details or incidents.

   3.5. The order in which the details or incidents are presented.

   3.6. The emphasis.

4. *Verbal part:* Explain the function of language in lending the poem the linguistic characteristics it possesses. If a particular poem arouses pleasure through sound effects, then identify the devices of language (rhyme,

meter, or whatever) that arouses such responses. If a poem is a unified whole, explain how language contributes to that unity. If a poem depicts what it does succinctly, then identify the linguistic means through which such succinctness of expression is achieved. Guard against holding preconceived notions of what the language of poetry is supposed to be like. Instead, assume that the task of the verbal part directs readers to discover, without preconception, just how it functions to produce the effects.

PART-WHOLE SKILLS FOR COMPREHENDING POEMS ORGANIZED BY ARGUMENTS

1. *Purpose:* Identify the intended emotional effects as well as the intended informative, persuasive, or other rhetorical effects to be produced upon the audience. Justify this judgment by explicit references to the text.
2. *Form:* Identify the explanation or argument that is related to the purpose or effects. State relations between the main explanation or argument and the effects sought.
3. *Nonverbal parts:* (Same as section 3 in the preceding table).
4. *Verbal parts:* (Same as section 4 in the preceding table).

ness of expression, that implies the question, "Through what devices of language does the poem depict what it does briefly and compactly?" If the poem arouses pleasing sound effects, ask "Through what devices of language are pleasing sound effects produced?" And so on.

Significance

We are able to respond appropriately to this poem because we share the value built into it: sharing another's restoration of happiness. If we don't hold that value, we are unable to respond properly. The poem, further, invites us to recall those occasions in which some unexpected instance helped overcome an earlier sadness.

The part-whole skills formulated

The part-whole skills are formulated in the two accompanying lists.

Pitfalls

Because the pitfalls section in Chapter 6 identifies some of those common to the teaching of literature generally, they apply also to this chapter. There are, however, distortions that are unique to poetry.

One of these, already mentioned in Chapter 6, is so widely practiced that it bears repetition: Disregarding the person and functions of the speaker and assuming, wrongly, that only what the speaker relates is the action to which we respond. A related mistake is a failure to clarify whether the speaker is directly addressing the reader of the poem or some other person or group.

Another widely practiced distortion concerns the language of poetry. In this violation of principle, figures of speech, rhyme schemes, metrical patterns, and the like are treated as discrete entities. These practices become dull pedantic exercises of limited usefulness. Inquiry into the language of poetry becomes worth doing when the language is treated as a functioning part of the whole. In this view, we note the nonverbal and verbal effects of the poem and then explain how the language works to produce those effects.

Summary

1. The part-whole skills constitute a complete inventory for the mode of comprehension this chapter dwells on.

2. The same set of parts appear in both simple and complicated lyrics organized by a represented action. A somewhat different set of parts appear in simple and in complicated lyrics organized by an argument. When the principal aim of teaching is knowledge of the parts and their uses in comprehension, it is feasible to use simple poems.

3. No one can predict just what questions and explanations a class will need. The teacher's best guidance is a clear understanding of poems as made things, the ends and means of the poem under study, and the achievements expected.

Exercises

Exercise 1

Select a lyric poem that you think students will like. Justify your selection. Explain how you would use that poem to teach literal-sense comprehension. State whatever background information you would supply and the vocabulary or other comprehension problems you would anticipate. Formulate the questions and ideal answers related to the literal-sense objective.

Exercise 2

Select a poem organized by a represented action suited to the secondary school. Assume that the class already knows the literal sense of what is going on in it. Formulate the questions and desired answers for teaching the skills of purpose, whole and nonverbal parts. You need not follow the order given in the table of part-whole skills. Identify the nonverbal parts and show how each functions to produce the effects.

Exercise 3

Following the same procedure of selection, choose another poem, but one with particularly striking verbal effects. State the questions you would ask and the desired replies for helping the students identify these verbal effects and the causes incorporated into the poem for producing them.

Exercise 4

Assume that the students' sheer enjoyment of literature is the overall aim. Collect ten poems that you think secondary-school students will enjoy. In making your choices, look through a number of anthologies; for example, *Spoon River Anthology* by Edgar Lee Masters (Macmillan) contains many poems that students like. Select carefully for intrinsic interest. Also identify poems likely to affect community mores and prejudices.

Note

1. From *The Poetry of Robert Frost,* ed. Edward Connery Lathem (New York: Holt, Rinehart and Winston, 1969).

CHAPTER 8

THE COMPREHENSION OF DRAMA AND FICTION

The chapter discusses the selection of works, censorship, literal-sense and part-whole comprehension, and significance as these apply to drama and fiction.

Some characteristics of plays and fiction

When students have studied the comprehension of expository prose and lyric poetry, and have profited from such work, they are ready for similar work with drama and fiction. Typically, plays, novels and much short fiction cover a wider range of argumentative and represented action than short lyrics do.

Plays are intended to be acted whereas fiction is intended to be read. Plays, therefore, produce their effects by what the audience can see and hear. The devices of drama include speeches, scenery, overt actions, gestures, costumes, and such signs as black armbands, Afro hairdos, and the like. These may be represented in a story or novel. But actions, speeches, and signs that are actually seen and heard are not available to fiction. The writer of fiction may, if he chooses, tell us what is in the minds and souls of his characters; he may tell his story from one or from varying points of view.

After students have worked systematically with the two literary kinds, they will have a basis for explicating these and other differences between the two. Because drama and fiction share a similar set of parts and similar degrees of magnitude, teaching to comprehend the two kinds may be viewed as a mutually supporting enterprise.

Distinguishing nonverbal parts in drama and fiction

Although the nonverbal parts of plays and fiction are similar, they are not the same. For one thing, fiction is made available through narration, but plays, through acting. It follows that plays do not have narrators in the same sense that fiction does. Narrations in plays are incidents, not means of representation. This matter is discussed in Chapter 6. Therefore, the narrator in a play is not a nonverbal part in the same sense that the narrator in fiction is. In plays, narrators and narrations are treated as incidents, another nonverbal part. In fiction and poetry the narrator or speaker is the means by which the work is represented.

For another thing, visual phenomena such as scenery, costumes, stage properties, and the like belong to plays and not to fiction. This book calls such visual matters, "spectacle." In plays, then, spectacle is a nonverbal part when it produces effects that clarify or move the action along. When dramatic incidents can be described without reference to spectacle, then spectacle need not be treated as a part, but considered only as a convention.

In the typical Shakespearian play, for example, references to spectacle need hardly be made in accounting for the action and effects. An example of spectacle as a part occurs in The Price by Arthur Miller. When the protagonist, Victor Franz, was young, he rationalized himself out of studying to become a scientist. He claims that there was no money then, a position he maintains even in his maturity. But the action brings out the possibility that the family's harp could have been sold to pay his expenses. On the stage, that harp occupies a prominent position from the opening to the closing curtains, thus reminding the audience of Victor's rationalization. In this instance, spectacle functions as a part.

A formulation of the nonverbal parts and the differences

between those of fiction and of drama appear in the table of part-whole skills, which is presented in this chapter.

Selecting works for teaching

Students enjoy and profit from their learning, and the right selection is a means to that end. Lyric poems are typically brief. If the class finds one to be dull, it can be conveniently and immediately dropped. Works of drama and longer fiction may require the purchase of a separate book, preferably in paperback. A classroom order of books is not easily set aside. Moreover, the study of a play or work of longer fiction requires more time. Considerable care, therefore, must be exercised in selecting these.

Nothing is more torturous for a teacher than trying to drag through a work (or through any activity) that the class finds distasteful. It is indispensable, therefore, that the students find the work interesting. If students find the work unbearable, then drop it immediately and without apology.

The inexperienced teacher may discover what students like by talking to their colleagues, by looking in school anthologies, and by examining the professional literature. Experienced teachers who know the students and their communities will be able to make wise selections independently. Students themselves may suggest titles, and they should be encouraged to do so. (Other suggestions for selecting works appear in Chapter 6.)

Classroom work psychologically belongs to the students if they are seriously involved in the selection of fiction and plays. The necessary evaluation of their suggestions and those of others must take into account (1) the extent to which the group as a whole is likely to be interested in the work; (2) the literary quality (we assume that the so-called "junior novels" have their uses, but that only works of reputable literary quality should be the primary objects of literary study); (3) cost (is the work available in low-cost paperback or otherwise conveniently accessible?); and (4) the probable acceptability to the community.

This fourth criterion requires further explanation. The objectives for the comprehension of literature may profitably and pleasurably be achieved through a wide variety of poems, plays, stories, and novels. Objectives specific to literature do not require works that a community finds offensive. Indeed, when tension surrounds the study of a literary selection, the classroom environment that results defeats efforts to learn.

This does not imply that the study of literature be limited to such socially inoffensive selections as *Macbeth* and *Silas Marner*. Communities vary widely in what they deem acceptable; today even conservative ones increasingly demonstrate enlightened attitudes. Before deciding on a work, consult with colleagues and administrators who know the community. The school literary anthology is almost always innocuously safe. Should problems of censorship arise, the school would be well advised to follow the procedures described in the NCTE pamphlet, *The Students' Right to Read*.

Assuming that a suitable work has been selected, I will now consider means for teaching students to get the literal sense of what is going on in a play or a work of fiction.

Teaching literal sense

I take as an example a play, *The Glass Menagerie*, by Tennessee Williams. It is particularly suited to secondary school students: It portrays conflict between generations, and to a lesser extent a bittersweet, unrequited love. Students are interested in such matters. It requires for its understanding knowledge that a typical adolescent already possesses. Some minor details, however, will need explaining. The play also provides suitable transition from the study of poetry already described.

In a sense, *The Glass Menagerie* is similar to some lyric poems: The play has a narrator, Tom Wingfield, by nature a poet. As a whole, the play is Tom's recollection and contemplation of an experience that he has undergone. The recollection and contemplation of experience, the students will recall, is typical to lyric poetry.

When students venture upon a long or fairly long work, it is a good idea for the teacher to help them get started. First, they may be asked to read and discuss the initial description of the scene, here the Wingfield apartment. Some vocabulary in the description is likely to cause trouble. The teacher's brief, straightforward explanation will suffice. With anticipated vocabulary problems cleared away, ask them to read the next two-page description of the scene and to be able to describe what the scene looks like. When they have finished the reading, discuss the scene. If a student's comments reveal miscomprehension, lead him back to the text so that he may correct himself.

To help them find their way into the action, read Tom's opening speech orally while the class follows along in their texts. Discuss briefly the family's situation—help the students see that the family is poor and in an ugly, demeaning environment, that the father has left them, and that Tom, his sister, and his mother constitute the family living in the apartment. Ask them how the play conveys that knowledge to them. Point out that Tom is "dressed as a merchant sailor." Ask what we are to infer from that. (He has left the family and gone to sea.) Then skip a few lines and read, preferably with a Southern dialect, natural or invented, Amanda's admonition to Tom and his reply:

Amanda [To her son]

Honey, don't *push* with your *fingers*. If you have to push with something, the thing to push with is a crust of bread. And chew—chew! Animals have secretions in their stomachs which enable them to digest food without mastication, but human beings are supposed to chew their food before they swallow it down. Eat food leisurely, son, and really enjoy it. A well-cooked meal has lots of delicate flavors that have to be held in the mouth for appreciation. So chew your food and give your salivary glands a chance to function!

[Tom deliberately lays his imaginary fork down and pushes his chair back from the table.]

Tom

I haven't enjoyed one bite of this dinner because of your constant directions on how to eat it. It's you that makes me rush through meals with your hawk-like attention to every bite I take. Sickening—spoils my appetite—all this discussion of—animal's secretions—salivary glands—mastication![1]

Ask what effect Amanda's speech is likely to have on Tom. (Disgust him.) Ask them what these two speeches do. (Make it plain that Tom and his mother don't get along. Make it probable that Tom, like his father, will leave the family.)

To this point, the classwork has been aimed at helping the students begin to realize what the scene may look like, how the dialogue may sound, and what kind of people Tom and Amanda are. This beginning sends them on their way to reading the play themselves. Guide them in their reading by suggesting that they be prepared to explain the following: By the end of the play Tom leaves his mother and sister. Describe the sequence of events that leads to his leaving. Ask them to use the remainder of the period to begin their reading and to have the entire play read by the next meeting of the class. When the class meets next, ask them to describe the sequence of events that led to Tom's leaving. The discussion will reveal a range of defensible and less defensible conceptions of what is literally going on in the play.

Hold the discussion with books open, and insist that statements be justified by explicit reference to the text, particularly to apposite speeches and stage directions. Ideally, free and responsible comment characterizes the discussion. If possible, supplement these activities with recordings. In one recording, Williams himself reads the beginning and ending passages of the play (Caedmon, TC 1005). Another record (Caedmon, TRS 301 M S) presents the play as a whole.

The students are likely to say that the action consists of the sequence of incidents that go on in the Wingfield apartment. The text makes it clear, however, that it's a "memory play," that everything in it is Tom's recollection, and that it is to Tom's recollection that we respond. In this play, then, there is complete congruence between the action and what is depicted on the stage.

Generalizing literal-sense procedure

From the foregoing discussion, we may infer that the teaching of literal-sense comprehension implies these tasks:

First, discuss the work as a whole and in its entirety whenever possible.

Second, anticipate difficulties students are likely to have with vocabulary, concepts, topical references, and the like. Explain these. The explanation need be no more complicated than that required for comprehending the work.

Third, help the class realize clearly how the work begins: the opening scene, the characters, and any other important issue or problem implied by the opening situation.

Fourth, frame a problem or question that students are to be prepared to resolve after they have read the entire work. The problem or question should direct their attention to concerns that are central to the work—for example, the sequence of incidents that make a final outcome necessary or probable.

Fifth, conduct a discussion through which students may clarify their comprehension of the literal sense of what is going on in the work. The discussion of the overall question or problem just referred to makes a suitable beginning.

This early phase in the study of literature should stress literature as a source of enjoyment. The short story is particularly suited to this aim because there is an abundance of stories that may be read and discussed within a single class period. Search the shelves of libraries and the displays of bookstores for the new and the different. Read many of these stories orally to the class. Have many on hand and read only what they find interesting.

Before reading, have them clear their desks, put pens and pencils aside, and give complete attention to the story and to the main question to which they are to respond. The class should understand that time allotted to listening is not to be used for doing homework in algebra. Keep the atmosphere purposeful, yet friendly and relaxed.

Teaching part-whole comprehension

As noted, part-whole comprehension refers to the process of identifying effects and identifying and explaining the causes or parts incorporated into the work for producing the effects.

I shall explain and illustrate this process with an especially brief short story.

Birthday Party

They were a couple in their late thirties, and they looked unmistakably married. They sat on the banquette opposite us in a little narrow restaurant, having dinner. The man had a round, self-satisfied face, with glasses on it; the woman was fadingly pretty, in a big hat. There was nothing conspicuous about them, nothing particularly noticeable, until the end of their meal, when it suddenly became obvious that this was an Occasion—in fact, the husband's birthday, and the wife had planned a little surprise for him.

It arrived in the form of a small but glossy birthday cake, with one pink candle burning in the center. The headwaiter brought it in and placed it before the husband, and meanwhile the violin-and-piano orchestra played "Happy Birthday to You" and the wife beamed with shy pride over her little surprise, and such few people as there were in the restaurant tried to help out with a pattering of applause. It became clear at once that help was needed, because the husband was not pleased. Instead he was hotly embarrassed, and indignant at his wife for embarrassing him.

You looked at him and you saw this and you thought, "Oh now, don't be like that!" But he was like that, and as soon as the little cake had been deposited on the table, and the orchestra finished the birthday piece, and the general attention had shifted from the man and woman, I saw him say something to her under his breath—some punishing thing, quick and curt and unkind. I couldn't bear to look at the woman then, so I stared at my plate and waited for quite a long time. Not long enough, though. She was still crying when I finally glanced over there again. Crying quietly and heartbrokenly and hopelessly, all to herself, under the gay big brim of her best hat.

Katharine Brush[2]

In the discussion that follows, the subheads are suggestive of questions; the material following the subheads gives explanation and ideal replies.

What is it?

"Birthday Party" is a represented action. It presents a moment of human experience that arouses emotional and other responses. The story is not an argument in fiction such as a fable, because there is no reason for us to suppose that its intention is to teach husbands to be nice to their wives or to admonish married couples to understand each other. Nor is it a psychological case study. The reader, we may assume, possesses the moral and psychological knowledge required for comprehending the story, and his possession of such knowledge is prerequisite to his responding appropriately.

What does it do?

The story is intended to arouse in the reader a feeling of sympathy. Pain rather than pleasure is the main effect. As Aristotle has shown, however, in represented actions, unlike in everyday life, the ugly and the painful are sources of pleasure.

What does it depict?

To arouse a painful effect in the artistic sense, a story must present an action that a qualified reader will find painful. The author of "Birthday Party" has chosen to present the following: A narrator recollects an incident in which a husband and wife, dressed for an occasion, are having dinner in a restaurant on his birthday. As a surprise to her husband, the wife has a birthday cake brought to their table, and the violinist and pianist in the restaurant play "Happy Birthday," after which the few other diners applaud. To all this, the husband responds with embarrassment and anger. Disappointed and heartbroken, the wife cries.

How or through what nonverbal parts is it depicted?

This imagined human action consists of a recollection of one particular narrator. The narrator, however, could have been the waiter, the busboy, the husband, the wife, or anyone else. In such an instance, the action would be different because it would be viewed from a different perspective.

The narration consists of the nonverbal parts. These are listed in the table. The nonverbal parts are embodied in language, which in this book is called the verbal part.

An explanation of the particular nonverbal parts incorporated into the story appears in the following four sections; the headings of these sections are Narrator, Details, Order, and Emphasis.

Narrator

The narrator is observant, articulate, sensitive, and a woman. We infer that she is observant from noting the telling observations of the couple and the setting; we infer that she is articulate from noting clear, vivid, and economical depiction; we infer that she is sensitive both from the foregoing and from noting her empathy for the wife's suffering when she says "I couldn't bear to look at the woman . . ."; we infer that the narrator is a woman from a preoccupation with the wife's hat and from the utterance, "Oh, now, don't *be* like that," which is language typically expected of women rather than of men.

Because our response depends upon our understanding a woman's disappointment and humiliation, the selection as narrator of an observant, articulate, and sensitive woman is appropriate. Moreover, the selection of such a narrator gives a feeling of trust in what is being told, and of admiration caused by our noting the keenness of observation and the economical and skillful use of language and detail.

It is important also to notice the time of narration with respect to the experience. That the narrator recalls the experience rather than describes it as it occurs conveys a sense of settled and considered judgment and therefore of confidence in what is depicted.

Having noted the character of the narrator, the time of narration, and the suitability of all this to the effects, we now consider the attitudes the narrator conveys. In this story, her attitude toward herself is hardly shown because the story doesn't require it. Her disapproving attitude toward the husband is hinted by the reference to his "self-satisfied face with glasses on it," and her sympathy for the wife is shown by references to the wife's fading beauty, thoughtfulness toward her husband, and final humiliation. The narrator's attitude toward the reader is made clear by the sentence in which she addresses the reader directly: "You looked at him and you saw this and you thought . . . " The narrator feels that the reader is her intelligent, perceptive peer who shares her feelings. This device of flattery, however, does not imply that we respond entirely as the narrator does; as will be shown, we shall see that the wife is not entirely blameless.

Details

The details have already been presented under the headings, "What is depicted?" and "Narrator." Briefly, part of our admiration of the story stems from the plot's being depicted by a representation that gives only a minimal but apposite set of details.

Order

Because we are to be affected by an incident, the order of presentation follows "real life," or chronological order. All human experiences, whether actual or imagined, occur chronologically. But real life order need not determine how the experience is represented to the audience. If an experience is not told in chronological order, it is always restatable chronologically.

Emphasis

The narrator has emphasized the cruelty of the husband to his wife. Because the main effect is our sympathy and pity for the wife, this emphasis is one means to that end. There is, moreover, a further device of intensification: We expect the husband to appreciate his wife's thoughtfulness; instead, his behavior is opposite to that which we expect.

In this story, emotional intensity, rather than amount of space, conveys that emphasis. Most of the space is devoted to a description of the restaurant and the couple. This is the setting for the husband's anger, the wife's disappointment, and, as a result, the reader's emotional response. Although amount of space is one device for emphasizing, it is not the only one. We infer emphasis by deciding what is most striking, and we account for emphasis by identifying the cause within the text of the striking effect.

Significance

Our painful response is aroused because our opinion of the action is one of disapproval. The values built into the story are those of mutual understanding, particularly between husbands and wives. In the story the mature and "unmistakably married" couple failed at this mutual understanding and this makes us disapprove. The husband should have been more tolerant than he was, and by this time the wife should have known her husband's idiosyncrasies. Both, therefore, demonstrate behavior that is below the level expected of mature adults. We therefore disapprove and this affects our emotional response.

Individualizing the reading of novels and plays

The literal-sense and part-whole skills for reading short stories are in principle the same as for reading novels. As mentioned, there are difficulties in finding a novel that all students will find appealing. Therefore, a teacher may find it expedient to encourage each student to read a novel of his own choice after he has learned the principles of reading fiction through classroom work in the short story. The relationship between one-act and full length plays is the same as that between short stories and novels.

In Chapter 6 I suggest some ideas for helping each individual select works that appeal. With the right novel or play selected and skills in the principles of comprehension acquired, each student may be set to work studying his novel or play in some systematic fashion. The table of part-whole skills provides a comprehensive list that may guide each individual's reading.

The guidance and evaluation of creative writing

This task is most directly and conveniently accomplished through the evaluation of the work of the student-writer and the discussion of the evaluation. That procedure makes it convenient to help the student write a work that he himself consciously or unconsciously seeks to construct.

In evaluating a piece of creative writing, then, a desirable practice would be the use of criteria by which the student-writer's selection could be judged not by abstract, preconceived notions of the characteristics the selection should possess, but rather, by the effects the work is designed to produce and the parts incorporated into the work for producing these. Evaluation, then, would include arriving at judgments about the extent to which the student writer has made the best possible use of the means he has selected; the principles of comprehension are also criteria for such evaluation. These principles are formulated in the two accompanying tables.

Pitfalls

The pitfalls cited in the two preceding chapters apply to this one as well. In addition, there are distortions characteristic of the teaching of fiction and drama.

When such works are organized by a represented action, it is all too common for the action to be equated with its representation. As Chapter 6 has shown, the action and its representation on the page or on the stage do not always correspond. Further, the represented actions of novels, plays, and some short stories are longer and more complicated than the actions of lyric poems. The teaching of drama and fiction, therefore, is misguided unless it is based on a clear and unambiguous idea of just what that action is.

Another degradation occurs when certain elements of fiction and plays are removed from their contexts and treated as discrete entities, often with a view to the specific teaching of morals. Thus, the platitudes of Polonius are cited as profound truths (e.g., "Neither a borrower or a lender be"), al-

PART-WHOLE SKILLS FOR COMPREHENDING PLAYS AND FICTION ORGANIZED BY REPRESENTED ACTIONS

1. *Purpose:* Identify the emotional effects to be produced upon the audience.
2. *Form:* State the main time-bound sequence of human experience or action through which the effects are produced. If there are subordinate sequences (subplots), identify these. Such experiences or actions need not be represented to the audience in chronological order, but the chronological order must be inferable and therefore statable. State the relation between the chronological sequence of action(s) and the intended effects.
3. *Nonverbal parts* (the representation): For works of fiction (a) identify each of the following and (b) explain its function in producing the effects. To do (a) but not (b) is to discuss separate topics, not the work as a unified whole. As a result of inquiry into the parts labeled 3.1 to 3.6, the reader should be able to explain what is presented (3.4), in what order (3.5), to what extent (3.6), and in what light (3.1 and 3.2). Because dramatic method requires acting upon the stage, delete 3.1, 3.2, and 3.3 but include the nonverbal part, which is spectacle. Refer to spectacle only when such visual matters are indispensable in explaining the action and effects of the whole.
   - 3.1. The kind of person the narrator is represented as being.
   - 3.2. The attitudes he conveys toward his audience, himself, and the experience he depicts. (Usually only one of these attitudes is dominant. Account only for the single dominant attitude.)
   - 3.3. The relation between the time of narration or representation and the time at which an action occurs.
   - 3.4. The set of details or incidents.
   - 3.5. The order in which the details or incidents are presented (in the representation).
   - 3.6. The emphasis.

PART-WHOLE SKILLS FOR COMPREHENDING PLAYS AND FICTION ORGANIZED BY ARGUMENTS

1. *Purpose:* Identify the intended emotional effects as well as the intended informative, persuasive, or other rhetorical effects to be produced upon the audience. Justify this judgment by explicit reference to the text.
2. *Form:* Identify the explanation or argument that is related to the purpose or effects. State the relation between the main explanation or argument and the effects sought.
3. *Nonverbal parts:* (Same as section 3 in the preceding table).

though these were written for particular dramatic purposes and, therefore, are properly judged in light of those purposes. This does not deny, however, that anyone who knows *King Lear* is not likely to be so imprudent as to give up his financial resources and entrust these to others.

Fiction and drama are particularly accessible to students who like to "identify with" and "relate to" what they read or see. As Chapter 6 has shown, such responses are at odds with a rational conception of literary study.

Summary

1. Drama and fiction represent their actions differently. But both forms permit longer and more complicated argumentative and represented action than short lyrics do. That shared element suggests why it may be convenient to treat drama and fiction together.

2. Because of the expense and the time required for teaching, considerable care must be exercised in selecting full-length plays and novels for a class.

3. The part-whole skills may be used to individualize the reading of full-length plays and novels and to guide creative writing.

4. Should problems of censorship arise, the teacher and the administration of the school would be well advised to follow the procedures recommended in *The Students' Right to Read,* an inexpensive pamphlet published by the National Council of Teachers of English.

Exercises

Exercise 1

The selection of works of literature need not be limited to anthologies and curriculum guides. Search libraries, bookstores, and other sources for a set of five short stories that you think students will like. The stories should appeal to an untracked class that includes students ranging in socioeconomic background from the son of a dishwasher to the daughter of an ITT executive. Your own experience will help and your course in Social Foundations of Education also may help in making selections. Each story should be short enough to be read orally and discussed within the class period. What other criteria would you use in making the selections? Justify these criteria. Identify the stories and justify your choices.

Exercise 2

What play would you select for the kind of class just described? Look in a good bookstore for individual plays available in paperback. Before making a decision read through the plays and anticipate difficulties with comprehension and a conservative community. Select a play that you think will fascinate the students yet not disturb the citizenry. Justify your selection. Next assume that you're going to use the play to teach literal-sense comprehension. Describe the steps you would take and why. Then assume that you're going to use the play to teach part-whole comprehension. Write out the questions you would ask, the replies you would expect, and justify replies by referring to the text of the play. Limit the discussion to effects, whole, and nonverbal parts. *Be sure to explain the functioning of each of the nonverbal parts.*

Exercise 3

Follow the procedures outlined in Exercise 2, but relate them to a short story or novel.

Notes

1. From *The Glass Menagerie* by Tennessee Williams (New York: Random House, 1973).
2. Originally published in *The New Yorker*, 22, No. 5 (March 16, 1946), 54.

CHAPTER 9

AN OUTLINE FOR THE STUDY OF LANGUAGE: SOME GROUND TO BE BROKEN

The study of language itself is distinguished from the widely accepted aspects of English, which are concerned with the uses of language. The topic is used to show how the analysis of ideas may be used to infer objectives from which coherent programs of instruction may be derived.

Distinguishing the study of language from the more familiar aspects of the English curriculum

The earlier chapters discuss, mainly, such familiar parts of English as the comprehension and writing of verbal discourses. In those discussions, I treat language as the material out of which such discourses are made. In this chapter, however, I treat language as an object of study. Both prospective and practicing teachers have difficulty with this kind of objective. An explanation, therefore, is required.

The general aim and its justification

By the study of language, I do not refer to the improvement of reading, writing, and speaking. Nor do I refer to punctuation, capitalization, the inculcation of correct usage, or to spelling as a practical skill; such matters are discussed in Chapter 5. Rather, by the study of language, I mean an understanding of such topics as these: properties of all human languages; descriptions of how the English language conveys meaning; social and geographical variations in the use of language; relations between speech and its representation in our everyday system of writing; lexicography; and the history of our language.

Why should such study be part of school learning? I would justify such study by the following line of argument: The starting point is the assumption that the broad purpose of education is increased knowledge of man and his world. It is obvious that language is second in importance to no other aspect of man and the world he lives in. Linguists have observed, however, that people in general, including the conventionally well-educated, are uninformed and misinformed about linguistic matters. Such misinformation results in dubious thought and action; for example: failure to learn a foreign language spoken in one's own home, failure to accept dialects different from one's own, confused thinking and discussion about speech and its relation to writing, and so on. Further, in typical English classes, the most widely used grammar lacks intellectual coherence and consistency; therefore, the discussion of language in general, and of the language in literary works in particular, lacks a rational basis.

Some difficulties to be overcome

The incorporation of linguistic study In schools faces several difficulties: One is a narrowly practical cast of mind that dominates classrooms in English. To be specific, over the years I have observed that typical students and teachers of English consciously or unconsciously hold to the belief that unless the study of language is directly related to improved speaking, writing, and comprehension, such study is impractical and a waste of time.

This narrowly practical attitude, I must point out, is not shared by our colleagues in other fields, particularly by those in mathematics and the sciences. In elementary and secondary schools these colleagues teach without apology and without references to uses in everyday living, the number system, the ideas behind the arithmetical processes, the solar system, the anatomy of a frog, and so forth. Such topics are taught from a conviction that they are intrinsically important.

A second difficulty is the lack of sound linguistic education of teachers and of those who teach them. Typical college and university departments of English are concerned mainly with literature and to a much lesser extent with composition. There are only a few good linguists in the nation and only a few of these instruct teachers of English. This emphasis affects the capabilities and interests of graduates of our English departments.

A third difficulty is different from the other two and is one that characterizes all lively empirical fields: Linguistics is in a constant state of change, with the result that the newer books and articles on syntax, for example, are outmoded before they reach print. I hasten to add that the ephemeral value of syntactic descriptions is not at all to be deplored; it is the price of forward movement.

A distinction must be drawn between ephemeral formulations and their underlying permanent principles. An example of a permanent principle is the following assumption of transformational grammar: The central characteristic of language is that speakers make and understand new sentences all their lives. An ephemeral formulation is a grammarian's explanation or set of rules that explains in part, and in some detail, this generative competence of speakers.

The teacher of English who would keep up with developments in the field of linguistics must, therefore, learn how to read the writings of linguists. The task implies the use of the analysis of ideas in reading linguistic writings.

Planning a unit of instruction

Having suggested the values of linguistic study and some difficulties that face it, I go on to suggest what can realistically be done. The discussion will make explicit the procedures by which a teacher may move from an analysis of scholarship, particularly the more or less permanent principles, to work in the classroom.

This process of inquiry begins with the assumption that a particular field of study, in this case linguistics, may offer contributions to the education of everyday citizens who are not likely to become professional linguists. The job then, is to determine what linguistics has to offer to the education of typical citizens.

For example, I have already noted that the typical citizen ought to know something about human language because of its intrinsic importance. The proper primary source of such knowledge is the linguist. The next step is to analyze the ideas (Chapter 4) of reputable linguistic writings. Thus we identify the terms, distinctions, and methods of thinking, and so on that we may wish to teach.

With ideas, distinctions, and methods of linguistic inquiry identified, we then put to use our method of curricular inquiry, which is described in Chapter 1. The curricular method is a guide to these tasks: (1) translating the potential contributions of linguistics into statements of Level 3 and 4 objectives; (2) inferring activities by which students may acquire the learning specified by the Level 3 objectives; (3) determining a feasible order for presenting the learning activities; and (4) evaluating the achievement of students and, thereby, the success of the program.

The properties of human language

To illustrate the procedure just described, we may begin by accepting the argument stated earlier that our students need to know what language is. We assume that language is what reputable linguists say it is. An elementary knowledge of scholarship and human nature points to the belief that a single monolithic conception of human language will never be forthcoming. Therefore, we select one or more of these conceptions.

One such conception has been formulated by a scholar of unquestioned distinction, Edward Sapir. His familiar definition of language, while somewhat old-fashioned to some, is nevertheless informative and may therefore be presented as one of a number of responsible formulations. His definition follows:

Language is a purely human and non-instinctive method of communicating ideas, emotions, and desires by means of a system of voluntarily produced symbols. These symbols are, in the first instance, auditory and they are produced by the so-called "organs of speech."[1]

From this definition and our earlier discussion, we may derive the following as Level 3 objectives:

1. Explain the meaning of a definition of language.
2. Distinguish examples of language from other similar matters.

For achieving the first of these objectives, the following selection and organization of learning activities may be suggestive.

First, present the definition to the students and ask them to describe in one word just what Sapir means by language. Help them see that the words "auditory" and "so-called organs of speech" imply that the word "speech" indicates what language is to Sapir. With that clarified, suggest that an explanation of language, in this view, must be an explanation of the characteristics or properties of speech. The definition gives a set of terms that explains what these characteristics are. List these terms on the board or through overhead projection and then ask the students to infer from the context of the definition what each term means. The context of the definition may be found in Chapter 1 of Sapir's *Language: An Introduction to the Study of Speech.* Ask, for example, why Sapir included in his definition the term "purely human." (To distinguish speech from animal communication).

Such a discussion may be summarized by the list of terms together with a gloss for each that the class infers. The list may look something like this:

1. Purely human—animal communication is not an example of language.
2. Noninstinctive—instinctive, blood-curdling cries and yells, although they communicate, are not examples of language.
3. Method of communication—speech is not itself com-

munication, but is one of a number of methods of communication.

4. System—each language permits only a certain selection of sounds and only certain arrangements of its parts.
5. Symbol—words are symbols in the same sense that flags and crosses on churches are.
6. Auditory—in this view, language is auditory (speech), not visible (writing).
7. So-called "organs of speech"—in this view the tongue, teeth, lips, and so on are primarily organs of digestion and respiration and have only secondary uses in the production of speech sounds.

The discussion conveys to the student such ideas as these: that language is distinctively human, auditory, and is not to be confused with such similar matters as animal communication, communication in general, other symbolic systems, and instinctive outcries. Additional characteristics derived from other sources may be added to the definition. For example, the characteristic of arbitrariness, which holds that there is no natural, necessary, or logical relationship between an entity of language and the meaning it conveys.

Further, Sapir's definition may be contrasted with others, particularly with that of the transformationalists, who maintain that it is misleading to suppose that speech implies merely a secondary use of the organs used to produce speech: Humans, the transformationalists contend, are biologically and psychologically predisposed to the acquisition and use of language.

Teaching grammar

Here the word *grammar* does not refer to correctness, spelling, and the like; it means a description of how a language works. Usually, current introductory courses in linguistics inform their students that grammars of English follow differing modes of scholarship or grammatical description. One of these has been called "scholarly traditional" and is exemplified by the English grammars of George Oliver

Curme, an American; Otto Jesperson, a Dane; E. Kruisinga and H. Poutsma, Dutchmen; and Henry Sweet, an Englishman. American taxonomic or structural grammars have been written by Charles Carpenter Fries, Henry Lee Smith Jr., and George L. Trager; generative-transformational grammars are being developed by Noam Chomsky, Morris Halle, and others.² The kinds of grammar incorporated into typical widely used composition textbooks can hardly be called works of serious scholarship, and later I explain why. Throughout the book I hold to the principle that there should be no inconsistency between sound scholarship and school learning.

Because grammars describe how languages work, I suggest as a Level 2 objective, "Understand how the English language works." Each grammar conveys its own notion of "understand." If, for example, we are teaching a generative-transformational grammar, the following Level 3 objectives would be implied: "Explain in specific detail some of the knowledge that permits speakers of English to make and understand new sentences all their lives." Similarly, the teaching of a taxonomic or structural grammar would be aimed at the students' ability to "Identify the formal signs within a sentence wherein the meanings are carried."

Apart from these generalized notions about teaching a particular grammar, there is a body of grammatical knowledge that is widely accepted by all or at least most schools of grammatical analysis. It is accessible in reputable grammars,³ but unfortunately it is generally misunderstood or not understood by both average and excellent secondary-school students as well as by the conventionally educated public. The purpose of such teaching may be expressed generally as the following Level 2 objective: "Grammatical literacy" or "Responsible understanding of English sentence structure." Related to these are the following Level 3 objectives:

1. Distinguish derivational endings from inflectional endings.
2. Distinguish modal auxiliaries (*shall, should, may, might, must,* etc.) from other auxiliaries (*have, been, is, was,* etc.).

3. Explain the fact that the English language has no future tense in the sense that French and Spanish have future tenses.
4. Distinguish transitive from intransitive verbs.
5. Explain relationships and lack of relationships between grammatical tense and chronological time.
6. Explain the "perfect" forms of verbal phrases.
7. Explain the "progressive" forms of verbal phrases.
8. Explain the relationships between active and passive forms of sentences.

And so on.

For carrying out the instruction, the requirements are a piece of chalk and a linguistically informed teacher. Through explanation and discussion the teacher imparts the grammatical principle or concept: derivation and inflection, for example. He provides the students with words and sentences by which they identify concepts and apply principles. (Which of these words have derivational endings? Which have inflectional endings? Justify your decision.) The results expected of such activities are students able to discuss grammatical matters and English sentence structure with some precision and responsibility, and able, also, to comprehend and criticize the writings of grammarians. The history of grammatical inquiry, even to the present day, supports Sapir's observation that all grammars leak.

Grammar and the analysis of ideas

The foregoing discussion suggests that the analysis of ideas (Chapter 4) is indispensable to the intelligent teaching and learning of a grammar: When Chomsky asserts that a grammar is a limited set of rules that represents what a speaker knows about his language, he is using *grammar* in a sense quite different from the grammarian who describes a language by noting the bits, pieces, and machinery of particular stretches of speech.

Our reference to widely used schoolroom grammars suggests another sense in which the analysis of ideas may contribute to grammatical study. The schoolroom tradition tells us, for example, that a sentence expresses a "complete thought." No one will argue, however, that "it is" is a sentence, although what the thought is and whether it is complete are questions that no one is likely to resolve.

For another example, a definition of *subject* traditional to the schoolroom is "what the sentence is about" and *predicate* is a "statement made about the subject." The definition is seen to be ridiculous when we realize that in the sentence, "boys run," the sentence is just as much about *run* as it is about *boys,* and the word *boys* makes a statement about *run,* just as *run* makes a statement about *boys.*

For another example, consider the schoolroom definition, "a preposition shows a relationship between its object and some other word in the sentence." If we take this definition seriously, we are forced to conclude that in the sentence "I like fish," *like* is a preposition because it shows a relationship between its object, *fish,* and another word in the sentence. Such ludicrous definitions partly explain why typical schoolroom grammar lacks intellectual respectability.

I am suggesting, then, that grammatical study may very well include the criticism of grammars. The widely used schoolroom grammars may, therefore, serve as handy materials with which to begin.

The function of language in connected discourse

Definitions of language often include explanations of linguistic functions or uses. Sapir's definition, cited above, is an example. Such definitions usually neglect to point out that in a serious sense, the language is the least important part of a verbal discourse. Our discussion of part-whole comprehension provides background for teaching this aspect of language. We may begin by discussing with students the principles upon which verbal discourses are constructed. Ask them to recall that the purpose of a discourse determines what the discourse consists of. If, for example, an editorial is intended to persuade the readers to vote for candidate X, then the discourse must consist of an argument to that effect. If such an argument is made available to the reader, it must be presented through the nonverbal parts, which must be embodied in particular language or words, the verbal part.

These principles of construction make clear that effects or purpose determines the argument. Purpose and argument determine the nonverbal parts. And purpose, argument, and nonverbal parts determine the language. But the language determines nothing else in the discourse. Put another way, language is the least important principle by which discourses are constructed. In another sense, however, it is the most important part, because access to verbal discourse is provided only by language.

The kind of discussion just suggested may explain why it is that a kind of literary criticism or discussion that is largely or exclusively concerned with the language of discourses is not likely to be very informative about problems of effect, action and nonverbal parts. Further, in teaching comprehension and writing, learning activities dealing exclusively with language are likely to be of dubious value for the same reason: A failure to inquire into the principles of construction that determine what the language must be or ought to be.

Extending the linguistic curriculum

I have illustrated a procedure by which a teacher may develop a curriculum for the study of language or for the study of anything else. The procedures may be expressed as a five-step process, which we may call "The Process of Innovation" because the process applies to the incorporation into the curriculum of any aspect of scholarship.

We may use this five-step procedure, then, to extend the linguistic curriculum so that it may include dialectology, lexicography, history of the language, syntax, phonology, and the like. Briefly, as teachers of English, we may examine any subject within linguistics to infer its possible educational uses for ordinary citizens. The accompanying table presents the five-step process by which these or other unfamiliar topics may be incorporated into a curriculum.

A PROCEDURE FOR INNOVATING

1. Identify an educational need.
   Example: The need to understand what language is.
2. Identify the related scholarship.
   Example: Sapir's definition of language.
3. Analyze the ideas in the scholarship.
   Example: The terms and distinctions in Sapir's definition.
4. Infer Level 3 objectives.
   Example: "Explain the meaning of a definition of language."
5. Select, organize, and evaluate learning activities.
   Example: See the discussion of the selection and organization of learning activities in Chapter 1. See Chapter 3 for procedures and examples of evaluation.

Pitfalls

Popular opinion about the teaching of English holds that linguistic and grammatical topics exist to improve the use of language. When that opinion is accepted and its consequences carried out, the distortion that results is the study of linguistic content for objectives that are inappropriate to it. The skills of grammatical analysis, for example, are hardly appropriate means to improved speaking and writing.

For another example, no one needs to study lexicography to know how to use a dictionary. Rather, lexicography explains the purposes and methods of making a dictionary. Similarly, knowledge of our everyday writing system sheds light on its properties, but the knowledge is not prerequisite to better writing.

Summary

1. No other possession of man and society is more important than language. That justifies the study of linguistic topics in the English curriculum.

2. Narrowly-practical attitudes typical to the teaching of English hinder proper instruction in linguistic topics. So does dubious education of teachers in reputable grammars and in such other linguistic topics and methods as dialectology, lexicography, linguistic history, and so on.

3. To innovate interesting, coherent, and sound programs of instruction, the teacher may use the following investigative methods: the analysis of ideas, methods of linguistic inquiry, and methods of curricular inquiry.

Exercises

Exercise 1

Read the chapter "The Dialects of American English" by Raven I. McDavid, Jr., in *The Structure of American English*, by W. Nelson Francis, or a similar discussion of dialects in America. Assume that you want your students to have an understanding of American dialects based on such scholarship. From an analysis of the ideas in the scholarly source, infer Level 3 objectives and a selection and organization of learning activities for developing the achievements specified by the objectives.

Exercise 2

Read a brief history of the English language that appears in one of the standard college dictionaries or in some other reputable source. Carry out the procedures cited in Exercise One for deriving objectives and the other aspects of instruction.

Exercise 3

The grammars of some intellectual respectability may be grouped into three kinds: (1) Scholarly-traditional, exemplified by the grammars of Jespersen, Sweet, and Curme; (2) Structural or taxonomic, exemplified by the grammars of Trager and Smith, Fries, and Francis; and (3) Transformational-generative, exemplified by the grammars of Chomsky, Halle, and their followers, popularizers, and deviators from their principles. The writings of these three kinds of grammarians are brought together in the book *English Linguistics: An Introductory Reader* by Hungerford, Robinson, and Sledd (Glencoe, Ill.: Scott, Foresman, 1970). Other sources are listed in notes to this chapter. (a) Select one of these kinds of grammar; (b) identify its assumptions and methods by reading the related article in *English Linguistics* or in another source; (c) reproduce a portion of its syntax and explain how this syntax incorporates or expresses the methods and assumptions of the grammar; and (d) explain the Level 3 objectives for teaching that grammar and, related to the objectives, the selection, organization, and evaluation of learning activities.

Notes

1. Edward Sapir, *Language* (New York: Harcourt, Brace, 1921), p. 8.
2. Noam Chomsky, *Aspects of the Theory of Syntax* (Cambridge, Mass.: M.I.T. Press, 1965). This and other publications in trans-

formational-generative syntax are dated. For teaching such a syntax, teachers may seek formulations of base or phrase-structure rules and transformational rules that seem to them to clarify their intuitions about English syntax.

3. George Oliver Curme, *Parts of Speech and Accidence* (Boston: D.C. Heath, 1935); Otto Jespersen, *Essentials of English Grammar* (New York: Henry Holt, 1933); Otto Jespersen, *A Modern English Grammar on Historical Principles* (7 vols.; Copenhagen: Einar Munksgaard, 1909–49); E. Kruisinga, *A Handbook of Present-Day English* (5th ed., 3 vols.; Groningen: P. Noordhoff, 1931); H. Poutsma, *A Grammar of Late Modern English* (Groningen: P. Noordhoff, Pt. I, 2nd ed., 1928–29; Pt. II, 1926); Henry Sweet, *A New English Grammar* (Oxford: Clarendon, Pt. I, 1891; Pt. II, 1898).

GLOSSARY

Achievement.   An *objective* refers to the learning of students that is intended or desired by a program of instruction. *Achievement* refers to the learning itself without reference to its being intended or desired. See *Behavior, Objective.*

Action.   This book uses *action* as a technical term, in its discussions of literature. Literary responses are produced by the reader's or spectator's observing a sequence of thoughts, emotions, overt activities, or any synthesis of these. Action refers to such sequences. In some contexts of this book, *action* is used in the same sense as *represented action.* See *Character, Represented action, Thought.*

Activity.   *Activity* is what a learner does, and should not be confused with *experience.* See *Experience.*

Analysis of ideas.   An argument exhibits a process of reasoning. Therefore, an argument may be comprehended for the reasoning that it exhibits. This implies a particular aim and method of comprehension; the method is called the *analysis of ideas.* Because all formulations of the arts, the sciences, and ideas on all topics are presented as arguments, the analysis of ideas is a method for inquiring into all subjects, problems, and issues.

Argument.   The term *argument* means a verbal discourse intended to persuade. It may vary in complexity from "Cigarette smoking may be dangerous to your health" to the Declaration of Independence. Not only are arguments presented in expository prose, they are also presented in certain works of poetry, drama, and fiction. See *Argumentative action, Exposition, Represented action.*

Argumentative action. In poems, plays, and fiction organized by arguments, the action functions as proof of the thesis or doctrine argued. This book calls such an action argumentative and distinguishes it from a represented action.

There are three kinds of proof and, correspondingly, three kinds of argumentative action: (1) inductive, in which the characters are presented as individuals and the audience generalizes from their actions, as in Ibsen's *Ghosts;* (2) deductive, in which the characters are presented as generalizations and the audience particularizes from their actions, as in *Everyman;* and (3) analogical, in which the characters and action constitute a one-to-one correspondence to the doctrine, thesis, or moral, as in *Aesop's Fables.* See *Action, Represented action.*

Attitude. The author of an argument, the narrator of a story or novel, and the speaker of a poem are represented in the works they depict as possessing particular personal characteristics. They are represented, also, as possessing feelings or tendencies to respond. Such feelings or tendencies are called attitudes. Attitudes arise from what is taken to be good or from what is valued. Therefore, attitudes imply values. In "Stopping by Woods," for example, the speaker's attitudes are admiration of beauty and commitment to responsibility, with responsibility winning out. These attitudes imply his values. See *Four causes, Nonverbal parts, Representation (of author, narrator, speaker).*

Audience. *Audience* refers to the recipient of a discourse or performance, and in a related sense means the person(s) spoken to in a literary work. In "To His Coy Mistress," for example, the speaker does not directly address the reader of the poem but, rather, his mistress. The understanding and teaching of such a work require that a distinction be drawn between the audience (here the mistress) and the reader of the poem. See *Part-whole comprehension, Qualified reader.*

Author. There are speakers of poems, narrators of fiction, and, analogous to these, *authors* of expositions and arguments in non-fiction prose. See *Narrator, Speaker.*

Behavior. Any example whatsoever of a human being thinking, feeling, or doing is an example of *behavior*. Because the purposes of instruction are particular desired changes in people's thinking, feeling, and doing, the objectives of instruction are the desired changes in the behavior of learners. See *Activity, Objective.*

Cause. The term is used here in two senses. In one of these, *cause* refers to a part incorporated into discourses by which effects are produced. Such causes are the nonverbal and verbal parts. *Cause* is also used in the sense of the necessary determinants by which things are made and activities performed. These determinants explain things and activities in terms of their purposes, forms, making or doing, and materials; expressed more traditionally, the final, formal, efficient, and material causes are used to explain and understand actions and things. See *Four causes, Nonverbal parts, Part, Verbal part.*

Character. In discussions of represented actions, *character* refers to good and bad, virtue and vice, and so on as preferences of people that lead to action, which in turn affect our emotions. See *Action, Represented action, Thought.*

Comprehension. *Comprehension* means the process of understanding verbal discourses and plays, and is distinguished from *inference.* The skills of understanding are inferred from the properties of such discourses. A discourse, for example, has the property of saying something literally; it may be understood, therefore, as literal statement. That skill is called *literal-sense comprehension.* A discourse also has the property of affecting readers; it may be understood, then, as a means to the producing of effects. The skills implied are called *part-whole comprehension.* Further, a discourse has the property of demonstrating a process of reasoning; this, it may be understood as a means for resolving a problem. The skills implied are called *analysis of ideas.* See *Analysis of ideas, Inference, Literal-sense comprehension, Part-whole comprehension.*

Criterion-referenced test. See *Criterion test.*

Criterion-related test. See *Criterion test.*

Criterion test. A *criterion test* is designed to identify what learners know or can do. In teaching and instruction generally, criterion tests are designed to determine the extent to which learners are achieving or have achieved the behaviors or achievements specified by the objectives of the program. Such terms as *criterion-referenced test* and *criterion-related test* are used in this same sense.

Curricular inquiry.   Any particular problem of planning and teaching entails one or some combination of the following: the justification, selection, and formulation of objectives; and the selection, organization, and evaluation of learning activities. *Curricular inquiry* means any systematic procedure for resolving a problem in planning and teaching which implies the use of the distinctions and relationships just noted. See *Activity, Evaluation, Objective, Organization.*

Effects.   Part-whole comprehension assumes that verbal discourses are intended to produce *effects* upon readers and audiences. The number of effects possible is equal to the number producible by language. Because purpose determines everything in a made thing, the effects of a discourse determine its form and its verbal and nonverbal parts.

The effects that a particular discourse actually produces upon a particular reader or member of an audience do not necessarily correspond to the causes of effects that are incorporated into the work. The causes are the nonverbal and the verbal parts. *Effects* refers to those effects whose causes are incorporated into the work. See *Nonverbal parts, Part-whole comprehension, Qualified reader, Verbal part.*

Efficient Cause.   See *Four causes.*

Ends.   *Ends* means purposes, but in a sense that requires further explanation. Purposes or ends of made things are never part of them. We may say, for example, that the purpose of a pencil is a written message. A written message, however, is not a part of the pencil. And so it goes for all made things including programs of instruction, arguments, poems, plays, and works of fiction.

In a program of instruction, the purpose is particular changes in what students are to know, do, understand, appreciate, and so on. But students' possessing these desired changes are not part of the program of instruction which is, essentially, a set of stimuli to which students are to respond. The responses of students (ends) exist apart from the stimuli (means). Because programs of instruction are means to desired changes within students, these desired changes must be known in some manner, certainly to teachers and, in the opinion of the writer, to students as well.

A spoken or written discourse, viewed as communicative, has as its purpose particular intended effects upon hearers and readers. But such intended effects cannot be a part of the discourse. Because made things are constructed to achieve their ends or purposes, intelligent thinking and teaching of verbal discourses require that the ends or effects to which the discourses are means must be known in some manner to teachers and students of English. See *Effects, Part, Part-whole comprehension.*

Evaluation. Evaluation is a process of determining the extent to which the objectives of a course or other unit of instruction have been or are being achieved. Some writers use the terms *formative evaluation* to refer to the evaluation of instruction before the program has been completed and *summative evaluation* to refer to evaluation of a program as a whole. Such terms do not appear in the text of this book.

Experience. The essential means of learning is not activity, but the result of the response to the activity, which is called *experience.* See *Activity, Curricular inquiry, Objective.*

Explanation. See *Exposition.*

Exposition (Expository). Exposition in this text refers to explanation and to prose that explains. Although this book refers to works that argue and works that explain, the validity of the distinction is arguable because the same set of parts are incorporated into works that this book calls arguments and explanations. Such works are manifested in poems, plays, and fiction as well as in expository prose. See *Argument, Argumentative action, Expository prose, Part.*

Expository prose. The term refers to exposition and argument in non-fiction prose. See *Argument, Exposition (expository).*

Final cause. See *Four causes.*

Formal cause. See *Four causes.*

Four causes. An understanding of a thing or an activity may be defined as knowing its purpose (final cause), form (formal cause), work of the maker (efficient cause), and material (material cause).
 For a lyric poem, the purpose is the effects to be produced upon the reader; the form is the poetic action or argument; the work of the maker corresponds to the construction of the nonverbal and verbal parts because the process of writing consists of the construc-

tion of those parts; the material is language or the verbal part. See *Action, Effects, Ends, Nonverbal parts, Part-whole comprehension, Process of writing, Verbal part.*

Grammar.   *Grammar* means a scholarly description of a language; the term does not refer to matters of usage in speech and writing. See *Usage.*

Inference.   Apart from its conventional meaning, *inference* is used to distinguish the comprehension of a discourse from such matters as opinions about it, values attributed to it, and consequences that it may imply. Such opinions, values, and consequences may be those of the reader or of anyone else. A profitable discussion of a text requires that this distinction be kept in mind. See *Comprehension.*

Learning activity.   See *Activity.*

Literal-sense comprehension.   The term refers to the process of identifying the main action in works organized by a represented action, and the main argument in works organized by an argument. Although this skill is fundamental to the understanding of a discourse, it is not simple. In some discourses and plays, complications in identifying the literal sense arise because of disjunctions between the action or argument and its representation in print or on the stage. See *Action, Argumentative action, Manner, Nonverbal parts, Part-whole comprehension.*

Manner.   In expository prose, poetry, drama, and fiction, the represented action or the main argument is made available to the reader or spectator through the nonverbal and verbal parts. The nonverbal parts are sometimes called the *manner, manner of representation, depiction,* and *scenario.* See *Argument, Argumentative action, Explanation, Nonverbal parts, Represented action, Verbal part.*

Mastery learning.   *Mastery learning* designates a program of instruction based on the assumption that about ninety per cent of typical students can learn what the course has to teach provided proper means are used.

Material cause.   See *Four causes.*

Means.   Some writers use *means* to refer to the language of verbal discourses. For that same purpose, this book uses *verbal part.* See *Manner, Nonverbal parts, Object, Part-whole comprehension, Verbal part.*

Moral. The term is used in two different senses: The first is to refer to the qualified reader's judgment of the action of a work; such moral judgments fall somewhere on a scale from disapproval to approval, contempt to admiration, and so forth. The second refers to such matters as didacticism. See *Qualified reader, Significance of literature, Value.*

Narrator. In this book, *narrator* refers to the person or persons telling the story in a work of fiction. Although narrators appear in the plays *Our Town* and *The Glass Menagerie,* such narrations are incidents within the plays. In fiction, however, narration is necessarily the manner by which the action or argument is presented to the reader. This book uses *speaker* to refer to the person represented as relating a lyric poem, and *author* to refer to the person relating an exposition or argument in nonfiction prose. See *Manner, Nonverbal parts, Representation (of author, narrator, speaker).*

Nonverbal parts. A verbal discourse consists of a set of *nonverbal parts* and a verbal part. In works other than drama, the nonverbal parts are these: the personal characteristics of the speaker, narrator, or author and the attitudes he conveys, as these characteristics and attitudes are revealed by the text of the discourse; the details, or incidents he presents; the sequence in which he presents these; and the extent to which he emphasizes any of these nonverbal parts. The nonverbal parts of drama are the same, but with two exceptions: (1) omission of the narrator and his attitudes and (2) inclusion of such matters of spectacle as scenery, costume, and acting. For an explanation of narrators in plays, see *Narrator* and the explanation of this topic in Chapter 6.

The nonverbal parts are also known by such terms as *manner, representation, manner of representation, depiction,* and *scenario.* Except for matters of spectacle, the nonverbal parts are embodied in language or the verbal part.

Accurately speaking, authors do not directly construct such wholes as arguments and represented actions or plots. Rather, they so construct the nonverbal and verbal parts that these constitute wholes and produce effects. See *Manner, Verbal part.*

Norm-referenced test. See *Norm-related test (Norm-related evaluation).*

Norm-related test (norm-related evaluation). A *norm-related test* is designed to determine not what students know or can do, but rather how one student compares with another on a set of test items or other tasks. Only when the items are means for identifying such differences among test makers can the test be described as norm-related. The terms *standardized test* and *norm-referenced test* are used in the same sense as *norm-related test*.

Object.   *Object* in a technical sense is not used in this book. The term is used by some writers who follow methods of inquiry similar to that of part-whole comprehension. Their use of *object* is similar to the use in this book of *represented action*. See *Represented action*.

Objective.   Because the purpose of teaching is to produce changes in what learners are to know, understand, do, appreciate, show interest in, and so on, such desired changes are the *objectives* of teaching. Objectives determine everything in a program of instruction. Therefore, the teacher's knowing what the objectives are and how to select or devise these is of first importance. This book identifies four degrees of generality at which objectives may be stated; these degrees can be used to conveniently reveal the relationship between instruction and the larger purposes of schools, and education generally. See *Curricular inquiry, Evaluation, Experience, Learning activity, Organization*.

Organization.   *Organization* is used in discussions of curricular inquiry. Typically, organization means the order in which learning activities are intended to occur, whether in a single unit of instruction or over a number of years. Also, the term is sometimes used to refer to relationships between learning activities in one or more courses or programs. For example, learning activities in English, social studies, art, and music may all be related to American literature. See *Activity, Curricular inquiry, Objective*.

Part.   The term appears in discussions of composition and part-whole comprehension. In this book, a *part* does not refer to sections into which a work is divided, but to a cause of effects. Thus, a part is either one of the nonverbal parts or the verbal part. See *Nonverbal parts, Part-whole comprehension, Verbal part*.

Part-whole comprehension.   This term refers to the process of understanding verbal discourses and plays through identifying their effects, the causes that produce these, and the relationships between these causes and effects. The causes are the nonverbal parts and the verbal part. See *Nonverbal parts, Part, Verbal part*.

Plot.   Although *plot* appears only briefly in the text of this book, the term is widely and variously used. Its varying senses limit its usefulness in explicitness of discussion. Writers following methods of inquiry similar to that of part-whole comprehension use plot in the same or a similar sense that *represented action* is used in this book. More specifically, such writers usually take plot to mean the main action in plays and fictions that are organized by represented actions. In this book, however, represented action is extended to include the action in nonargumentative lyric poems. See *Argumentative action, Represented action.*

Practical wisdom.   This term, taken from the cardinal virtues of classical antiquity, is sometimes translated as *prudence* and refers to the habit of ordering the right means to the end. It implies such qualities as judging human actions properly and sympathetically, feeling emotions that are consistent with such understanding and judgment, and acting in accordance with good judgment. It is assumed in this book that a person of *practical wisdom* is the qualified reader of literature. To judge a work of literary art, then, we must ask how a person of practical wisdom would be affected by it.

   Practical wisdom also has implications for the construction of arguments. Aristotle in his *Rhetoric* points out that to compel belief, the discourse must represent the speaker as practically wise, morally virtuous, and concerned with the welfare of his audience; these three characteristics constitute an exhaustive list. See *Qualified reader.*

Process of writing.   Because a written discourse is a whole consisting of parts, the process of writing must be that of constructing the nonverbal and verbal parts that constitute the whole.

   The process of writing is often confused with matters that are external to the construction of the parts. In this confused view, the process of writing is said to be whatever thinking, planning, feeling, or doing that individuals may associate with the process of writing as just defined. Such associated activities can be only accidentally related to the writing process. See *Nonverbal parts, Verbal part, Whole.*

Qualified reader.   The arts assume a perfection or at least an adequacy of the sense(s) they address; music is not addressed to the deaf nor are the visual arts addressed to the blind. Because a work of literature presents a human action and a human action is judged somewhere on a scale of bad to good, wrong to right, base to noble, and so on, literature addresses the moral sense and, therefore, assumes a perfection of that sense. A qualified reader is one who is able to perceive clearly, to judge properly, and to respond appropriately to the human action that a literary work presents. For example, the qualified reader responds with admiration to acts of nobility and with pity to instances of undeserved misfortune. He does not respond with glee to acts of cruelty nor with admiration to acts of sadism. See *Effects, Practical wisdom*.

Reader. See *Audience, Qualified reader*.

Representation. See *Manner, Nonverbal parts*.

Representation (of author, narrator, speaker). An article, essay, report, or similar explanation or argument unavoidably depicts its author as possessing personal characteristics. The kind of person the author actually may be, however, is not necessarily the person that a selection depicts. This book uses *representation of the author* to refer to the kind of person that the discourse implies its author to be.

Similarly, a poem or work of fiction depicts its speaker or narrator as possessing personal characteristics. To refer to the kind of person so depicted, this book uses *representation of the narrator* or *speaker.)*

One sign of a good work is that the person represented as its author, speaker, or narrator functions appropriately to produce its intended effects. Because of this function, such a representation is a nonverbal part of a discourse. See *Manner, Nonverbal parts, Part*.

Represented action. The term is taken from the writings of Sheldon Sacks. Here the term means the main action in poems, plays, and fiction that are not organized by an argument. When a work so depicts the human actions of thought, feeling, and overt activity that we respond mainly to these rather than to issues outside the work, that work is organized by a represented action. In this book, represented actions are distinguished from arguments in literary form. Thus, *Hamlet* is an example of a represented action, and *Everyman* is an example of an argument. See *Argument, Argumentative action, Plot*.

Responses to literature. Because a work of literature is a determinate whole consisting of parts, all of which function to produce particular effects, a response to literature must consist, at least, of the inferring of the intended effects as well as the whole and its parts by which the effects are produced.

Responses to literature are sometimes confused with what readers attest their responses to be. Such attestations are not necessarily responses to literature: because of misreading, lapses of attention, inadequate background and so on, it is unreasonable to suppose that such a testimony is necessarily a response to warranted comprehension of what appears on the page or on the stage. See *Effects, Nonverbal parts, Verbal parts, Whole.*

Significance of literature. The *significance of literature* refers to the ethical and moral values conveyed by, and incorporated into, a work of literature. See *Value.*

Speaker. This book follows the convention of referring to "speakers" of poems and "narrators" of fiction. Thus, a poem is made available to the reader through one or more speakers. Such a speaker may either address the reader directly or address someone or some group other than the reader. See *Audience, Representation (of author, narrator, speaker).*

Spectacle. *Spectacle* refers only to plays, particularly to acting, scenery, stage properties, costumes, and so forth. Usually, spectacle is simply a conventional expectation. As such it functions as a convention, and it may be called a conventional part. Spectacle functions as a non-conventional part only when it provides a significant clarification or enhancement of the action. See *Nonverbal parts.*

Standardized test. See *Norm-related test (norm-related evaluation).*

Thought. Some discussions of represented actions include the term *thought* in the sense of knowledge, perceptions, sensitivities, views of situations, and so on. The context of the term includes *character* and *action,* which appear as entries in this glossary. *Character, thought,* and *action,* as used in this book, make it convenient to discuss actual and imaginary human actions: A person may know what is right (thought) but prefer what is wrong (character), and perform an action that strikes us as admirable or one that strikes us as contemptible. Represented actions and human actions generally exhibit various syntheses of thought, character, and action. See *Action, Character, Represented action.*

Time-bound. See *Represented action.*

Usage. *Usage* refers to such matters as punctuation, spelling, capitalization, grammatical construction, and selection of vocabulary only as these relate to the construction of written or spoken discourse. Grammar and usage are not used as synonyms. See *Grammar.*

Value.   The term appears in discussions of literary response and significance. It is used in the sense of "what is taken to be good." Because literature presents human thoughts, actions, and passions, and we judge these by what we value, it follows that *values* are built into literary works and explain much of our response to these. For example, we respond with approval and sympathetic pleasure to "Stopping by Woods" because we share a value built into it: responsibility in meeting obligations. See *Significance of literature.*

Verbal part.   The language of verbal discourses is called the *verbal part.* Language is the material that such discourses are made of. The nonverbal parts, then, may be defined as whatever is made out of the language. An analogy may clarify: A five-room house, a whole, may be analogized to *Huckleberry Finn,* another whole. The materials of that house—wood, bricks, plaster, and so on— may be analogized to the verbal part. Thus, the kitchen of that house is like a nonverbal part, and the verbal part is like the materials it is made out of.

It is important to realize that it is the kitchen and its function within the whole that determine what the materials shall be. The materials do not determine the kitchen and its function.

Similarly, in *Huckleberry Finn,* one of its nonverbal parts is the personal characteristics of Huckleberry Finn. This nonverbal part and its function within the whole determines the language. The language determines nothing else. See *Nonverbal parts, Part-whole comprehension.*

Whole.   In following part-whole methods of inquiry, some writers use *whole* in the sense of everything that a work contains. In this book, however, *whole* refers to the action in works organized by a represented action and to the main argument in works organized by an argument. A whole consists of the nonverbal and verbal parts. See *Argument, Argumentative action, Part, Part-whole comprehension, Represented action.*

INDEX

215